easy vegetarian

easy vegetarian

simple recipes for brunch, lunch, and dinner

RYLAND
PETERS
& SMALL

LONDON NEW YORK

Designer Luis Peral-Aranda
Commissioning Editor Elsa Petersen-Schepelern
Editor Sharon Ashman
Art Director Gabriella Le Grazie
Publishing Director Alison Starling

First published in the United States in 2003.

This paperback edition published in 2007
by Ryland Peters & Small, Inc.
519 Broadway, 5th Floor
New York, NY 10012
www.rylandpeters.com

10 9 8 7 6 5 4 3 2

Text © Tessa Bramley, Ursula Ferrigno, Alastair Hendy,
Louise Pickford, Fiona Smith, Fran Warde, Lesley
Waters, and Ryland Peters & Small 2003, 2007
Design and photographs
© Ryland Peters & Small 2003, 2007

Printed in China

ISBN-13: 978 1 84597 493 0
ISBN-10: 1 84597 493 X

The hardcover edition is cataloged as follows:

Library of Congress Cataloging-in-Publication Data

Easy vegetarian : simple recipes for brunch, lunch,
and dinner / Tessa Bramley ... [et al.].
     p. cm.
  ISBN 1-84172-492-0   3854-9159   10/08
  1. Vegetarian cookery. 2. Quick and easy
cookery. I. Bramley, Tessa.

  TX837.E29 2003
  641.5'636--dc21
                              2003001017

Notes

All spoon measurements are level
unless otherwise specified.

Ovens should be preheated to
the specified temperature. If using
a convection oven, cooking times
should be reduced according to
the manufacturer's instructions.

Uncooked or partially cooked eggs
should not be served to the very
young, the very old, people with
compromised immune systems, or
to pregnant women.

Specialist Asian ingredients are
available in larger supermarkets
and Asian stores.

To sterilize preserving jars, wash
them in hot, soapy water and rinse
in boiling water. Place in a large
saucepan and then cover with hot
water. With the saucepan lid on,
bring the water to a boil and
continue boiling for 15 minutes. Turn
off the heat, then leave the jars in
the hot water until just before they
are to be filled. Invert the jars onto
a clean cloth to dry. Sterilize the lids
for 5 minutes, by boiling, or
according to the manufacturer's
instructions. Jars should be filled
and sealed while they are still hot.
All pickles and preserves should
be processed in a boiling water-bath
canner according to USDA
guidelines. For information, see the
website at:
http://hgic.clemson.edu/factsheets/HGIC3040.htm

contents

easy peasy

Vegetarian food has become more and more popular, and not just with those who have chosen to follow a completely meat-free diet. More and more of us are choosing to cut down on the amount of meat we eat and turning to more healthy vegetarian alternatives. But the popularity of vegetarian food is not just due to its healthy reputation. Modern vegetarian cooking has become increasingly delicious and inventive, belying its reputation a decade or so ago as dull, brown, and stodgy.

However, if you aren't a seasoned vegetarian cook then it can be daunting to cook without meat. Vegetarian food is often deemed to be time-consuming and difficult to prepare with the misconception that you must soak and boil legumes for hours on end or spend an eternity peeling and chopping vegetables. This book will dispel that myth. It has easy-to-follow recipes for everything from warming comfort food to fresh and invigorating salads, and from quick snacks to more glamorous ideas to serve at a dinner party.

So whether you are a dedicated vegetarian yourself, are looking for menu ideas to cook for your vegetarian friends, or simply want to eat more healthfully, this is the book for you.

brunch

1¾ cups milk

½ teaspoon ground cinnamon

2 tablespoons honey

GRANOLA

2 cups rolled oats

½ cup oat bran

1 cup mixed chopped nuts, such as hazelnuts, almonds, macadamias, and cashews

2 tablespoons sunflower seeds

2 tablespoons pumpkin seeds

2 tablespoons sesame seeds

⅓ cup raisins

⅔ cup mixed dried fruit, chopped, such as apricots, figs, dates, banana, and mango

TO SERVE

7 oz. fresh fruit and berries, about 1¾ cups

extra milk

SERVES 4

This is so yummy—a sticky, sweet, fruity dish made with a delicious granola mix, soaked overnight in cinnamon-infused milk. To serve, add whatever berries or other fruits take your fancy. If there is any granola left over, store it in an airtight container.

cinnamon-soaked granola
with fresh fruit

To make the granola, put the oats in a dry skillet over medium heat and cook, stirring, until toasted and golden. Repeat with the oat bran, nuts, and seeds, in separate batches. Let cool, then put all the toasted ingredients in a large bowl. Add the raisins and dried fruit and mix.

Put the milk, cinnamon, and honey in a saucepan. Heat until almost boiling, then remove from the heat.

Put the granola in bowls, pour over the hot milk, and let cool.

Refrigerate overnight and serve at room temperature, topped with fresh fruit, berries, and extra milk.

blackberry buttermilk pancakes
with apple butter

APPLE BUTTER

1 lb. tart apples

3 tablespoons brown sugar

a pinch of ground cinnamon

1 teaspoon freshly squeezed lemon juice

2 tablespoons butter

PANCAKES

¾ cup self-rising flour

1 teaspoon baking soda

3 tablespoons fine cornmeal

3 tablespoons sugar

1 egg, beaten

1½ cups buttermilk, at room temperature

1 tablespoon butter, melted

1 cup small blackberries

oil, for greasing

TO SERVE

light cream

extra blackberries

SERVES 6

Apples and blackberries are great together, and here a buttery apple sauce tops blackberry-dotted pancakes. You could replace the blackberries with blueberries or raspberries, if you prefer.

To make the apple butter, peel, core, and chop the apples. Put in a saucepan with the sugar, cinnamon, lemon juice, and 1 tablespoon water. Bring to a boil, cover, and simmer over low heat for 15–20 minutes until softened. Mash with a fork, add the butter, and heat through, uncovered, until thickened. Set aside to cool.

To make the pancakes, sift the flour and baking soda into a bowl and stir in the cornmeal and sugar. Put the egg, buttermilk, and melted butter in a second bowl and beat well. Stir the mixture into the dry ingredients to form a smooth, thick batter. Fold in the blackberries.

Heat a nonstick skillet over medium heat until hot, brush lightly with oil and pour in a little of the batter to form a small pancake. Cook for 2 minutes until bubbles appear on the surface. Flip and cook for a further minute until cooked through. Keep the cooked pancakes warm in a low oven while cooking the rest.

Serve the pancakes topped with a spoonful of apple butter, a little cream, and extra blackberries.

warm blueberry and almond muffins

1¾ cups all-purpose flour

1½ teaspoons baking powder

1 teaspoon apple pie spice

½ cup ground almonds or ¾ cup slivered almonds, finely ground in a food processor

¾ cup sugar

1 egg

1¼ cups buttermilk

4 tablespoons butter, melted

8 oz. blueberries, about 2 cups

2 tablespoons slivered almonds, chopped

12-cup muffin pan with paper muffin cups

MAKES 10

Muffins are quick and easy to prepare and make a lovely breakfast or brunch snack, especially when served warm with coffee.

Sift the flour, baking powder, and apple pie spice into a bowl and stir in the ground almonds and sugar. Put the egg, buttermilk, and melted butter in a second bowl and beat well. Stir into the dry ingredients to make a smooth batter.

Fold in the blueberries, then spoon the mixture into 10 of the muffin cups in the muffin pan until each one is three-quarters full. Sprinkle with the chopped almonds and bake in a preheated oven at 400°F for 18–20 minutes, until risen and golden. Remove from the oven and let cool on a wire rack. Serve warm.

There are few things more enjoyable than eating brunch or breakfast outdoors in the summer. This recipe was inspired by a dish discovered at a café in Balmoral, a pretty beachside suburb of Sydney. Breakfast is big in this city, with hundreds of cafés, bistros, and bars offering wonderfully light, healthy food to people *en route* to work. You could replace a handful of the blueberries with raspberries, if you like.

berries with honeyed yogurt

8 oz. fresh blueberries,
about 1½ cups

a strip of unwaxed lemon zest

a squeeze of fresh lemon juice

a pinch of ground cinnamon

2¾ cups plain yogurt
(not low-fat)

⅓ cup honey

SERVES 4–6

Reserve a few of the best berries for serving and put the remainder in a saucepan. Add the lemon zest, lemon juice, cinnamon, and 1 tablespoon water. Heat gently for about 3 minutes until the berries just start to soften slightly. Let cool.

Spoon the berries into glasses, then add the yogurt and honey. Top with the reserved berries and serve.

honey-roasted peaches
with ricotta and coffee-bean sugar

Grinding whole coffee beans with a lump of sugar is typically Italian and adds a delicious crunch to fresh, juicy peaches. This is a wonderful recipe, to be enjoyed on a warm summer's morning.

6 large peaches or nectarines

2 tablespoons honey

1 tablespoon coffee beans

1 tablespoon sugar

1½ cups chilled ricotta cheese or cottage cheese, drained

SERVES 6

Cut the peaches or nectarines in half and remove the pits. Line an ovenproof dish with parchment paper and add the peaches or nectarines cut side up. Sprinkle with the honey and roast in a preheated oven at 425°F for 15–20 minutes, until the fruit is tender and caramelized. Let cool slightly.

Put the coffee beans and sugar in a coffee grinder and grind very briefly, until the beans and sugar are coarsely ground.

Spoon the peaches or nectarines onto plates, top with a scoop of ricotta, sprinkle with the sugary coffee beans, then serve.

french toast and sautéed tomatoes

Everybody loves French toast. Topping it with sautéed tomatoes makes a juicy brunch snack. Sautéing tomatoes seems to intensify their flavor and the heat makes them soft and velvety—truly delicious when served on French toast.

4 eggs

¼ cup milk

4 slices bread

4 tablespoons butter

8 ripe or green tomatoes, halved

sea salt and freshly ground black pepper

SERVES 4

Put the eggs, milk, salt, and pepper in a large, shallow dish and beat well. Add the bread and let soak for 5 minutes on each side so all the egg mixture is absorbed.

Heat a large, nonstick skillet over medium heat. Add the soaked bread and cook over medium-low heat for 3–4 minutes on each side.

Melt the butter in a separate skillet. Add the halved tomatoes and sauté for 2 minutes on each side. Put the hot French toast on warm plates and serve topped with the sautéed tomatoes.

omelet *fines herbes*

As omelets are best eaten as soon as they come out of the pan, it's best to serve this for no more than two people. However, if you want to make this for larger numbers, simply multiply the ingredients accordingly.

6 free-range eggs

2 tablespoons freshly chopped mixed herbs, such as chervil, chives, marjoram, parsley, and tarragon

2 tablespoons butter

sea salt and freshly ground black pepper

a few extra chives, to serve

SERVES 2

Put the eggs in a bowl, add half the herbs, and salt and pepper to taste. Beat well. Melt half the butter in an omelet pan until it stops frothing, then swirl in half the egg mixture.

Sprinkle with half the remaining herbs. Lightly fork through the mixture a couple of times so that it cooks evenly across the base.

As soon as it is set on the bottom, but is still a little runny in the middle, transfer to a warm plate, folding the omelet in half as you go. Sprinkle with chives, salt, and pepper. Serve immediately and repeat with the remaining ingredients to make a second omelet.

appetizers and snacks

Fresh asparagus stir-fried with ginger, orange, soy sauce, cashews, and a sprinkling of sesame oil makes a very simple yet sophisticated Asian-style appetizer to grace the table when cooking for friends.

1 tablespoon peanut or safflower oil

1 lb. asparagus, about 16, halved

½ inch fresh ginger, peeled and cut into fine matchsticks

½ cup chopped cashews, toasted in a dry skillet

grated zest of 1 unwaxed orange

1 tablespoon soy sauce

1 tablespoon sesame oil

SERVES 4

ginger asparagus
with cashews

Heat the oil in a wok, add the asparagus and ginger, and stir-fry for 4 minutes.

Add the cashews, orange zest, soy sauce, and sesame oil and continue cooking for 1 minute. Transfer to warm plates and serve immediately.

pesto-stuffed portobello
mushrooms with roasted vine tomatoes

6 slices fresh white bread, crusts removed and discarded

½ cup fresh pesto

8 portobello mushrooms, stalks removed

olive oil, for brushing

about 2 lb. cherry tomatoes, preferably on the vine

sea salt and freshly ground black pepper

TO SERVE

salad leaves, such as baby spinach or arugula

¼ cup extra virgin olive oil

2 tablespoons balsamic vinegar

a handful of basil leaves

SERVES 8

A great cheat's appetizer: the pesto is store-bought, the mushrooms make instant containers, and the tomatoes do their artful bit with almost no prodding or encouragement from you. And the cooking? Just minutes, but it will look like you've been hard at work for hours.

To make the stuffing, put the bread in a food processor and blend to make coarse crumbs. Add the pesto, salt, and pepper and blend briefly. Put the mushrooms in a roasting pan, sprinkle with salt and pepper, then brush liberally all over with olive oil. Fill with the pesto stuffing mixture.

Add the cherry tomatoes to the pan and sprinkle them with salt, pepper, and some more olive oil. Roast in a preheated oven at 400°F for about 8 minutes, or until the tomatoes begin to burst.

To serve, put small bundles of salad leaves on 8 serving plates and sprinkle with the olive oil and balsamic vinegar. Add a stuffed mushroom and a share of the tomatoes to each plate, top with a few basil leaves, and serve.

These delicious little packages of spinach and creamy ricotta encased in crisp phyllo are originally from Morocco, but these days they can be found all around the Mediterranean, with countless variations.

spinach and ricotta phyllo pastries
with slow-roasted tomatoes

6 tomatoes, halved crosswise

12 oz. baby spinach, washed and dried, about 3 cups

6 oz. phyllo pastry

4 tablespoons unsalted butter, melted

8 oz. fresh ricotta cheese, about 1 cup

½ cup pine nuts, toasted in a dry skillet

sea salt and freshly ground black pepper

a baking tray

SERVES 6

First, prepare the slow-roasted tomatoes. Put the tomato halves skin side down in an ovenproof dish, spacing them so they do not touch. Cook in a preheated oven at 250°F for 2 hours.

Put the spinach in a large saucepan over medium heat. Cook, stirring, until all the leaves have wilted, about 5 minutes. Transfer to a large colander and let cool, while the excess liquid drips out.

Put a clean dishtowel on a work surface and place a sheet of phyllo on top. Brush with melted butter and layer 3 more of the sheets on top, brushing each with butter. Put the ricotta, pine nuts, cooled spinach, salt, and pepper in a bowl and mix. Spread the mixture over the phyllo, leaving a 2-inch border all around.

Starting with one long side, roll up the phyllo into a log shape, using the towel to help you roll. Lightly twist the ends to enclose. Brush all over with melted butter, transfer to a baking tray, and cook in a preheated oven at 350°F for 30 minutes until golden. Slice and serve with the slow-roasted tomatoes.

rice-paper packages
with dipping soy

12 rice-paper wrappers*

2 carrots, cut into matchsticks

6 scallions, cut into matchsticks

4 oz. bean sprouts, about 1 cup

leaves from a bunch of Thai basil

a bunch of watercress

1 tablespoon sesame seeds, toasted in a dry skillet

DIPPING SOY

2 tablespoons honey

1 tablespoon soy sauce

1 tablespoon teriyaki sauce

1 red chile, thinly sliced

MAKES 12

These are time-consuming but worth it, so enlist some help when assembling if you can. They can be made in advance then kept chilled, covered with a damp cloth and plastic wrap, until needed.

Soak the rice-paper wrappers in several changes of warm water until soft, about 4 minutes.

Gather up little mixed clusters of carrots, scallions, bean sprouts, basil, and watercress. Put a cluster of the vegetables in the middle of each of the softened wrappers. Sprinkle with toasted sesame seeds and roll up to enclose the vegetables.

To make the dipping soy, put the honey, soy sauce, and teriyaki sauce in a small bowl and mix. Add the chile and transfer to a small, shallow dish to serve with the packages.

*Note: Vietnamese dried rice-paper wrappers (*báhn tráng*) are sold in Asian stores. Sold in packages of 50–100, they can be resealed and kept in a cool pantry.

Fennel is a beautiful vegetable, and very versatile. You can roast it with other vegetables or serve it raw in a salad, finely sliced or chopped. The fennel bulbs come in two shapes—very slim and tall, or plump and round. Guess what: the slim ones are male and the plump ones female!

2 fennel bulbs

4 shallots, chopped

1 teaspoon sugar

3 tablespoons olive oil

1 garlic clove, chopped

1 inch fresh ginger, peeled and chopped

a bunch of scallions, sliced

1 tablespoon sesame oil

freshly squeezed juice of 1 lemon

½ teaspoon chilli powder

sea salt and freshly ground black pepper

SERVES 8

baked fennel
with shallots and spicy dressing

Cut off the bases of the fennel bulbs and trim the tops. Cut each bulb lengthwise into quarters and cut out the hard core. Put in an ovenproof dish and add the shallots, sugar, and 2 tablespoons of the olive oil. Mix well and bake in a preheated oven at 325°F for 30 minutes.

Put the remaining olive oil in a small saucepan, add the garlic and ginger, and cook over very low heat for 10 minutes. Add the scallions, sesame oil, lemon juice, chilli powder, salt, and pepper to taste. Gently bring to a simmer, then pour over the roasted fennel, mix well, and serve immediately with all the juices.

stuffed sweet peppers

4 Cubanelle peppers, halved lengthwise and seeded

1½ cups chopped mushrooms, about 8 oz.

5 oz. mozzarella cheese, drained and cut into large cubes

2 garlic cloves, chopped

3 tablespoons olive oil

3 oz. olives, pitted and chopped, ½ cup

½ tablespoon paprika

sea salt and freshly ground black pepper

a baking tray, lightly oiled

SERVES 4

Long, thin, sweet Cubanelle peppers are best for this dish. However, if they aren't in season, bell peppers can be used, though a little extra filling may be needed, as they tend to be larger.

Put the pepper halves skin side down on the oiled baking tray.

Put the mushrooms, mozzarella, garlic, oil, olives, and paprika in a bowl. Add salt and pepper to taste and mix well. Spoon the mixture into the pepper halves. Cook near the top of a preheated oven at 350°F for 30 minutes. Serve hot or warm.

Mozzarella is a fantastic Italian cheese which can be made from either cow's milk or buffalo milk. It has a beautiful creamy, soft texture which contrasts perfectly with the firmness of the potatoes and crunchy fennel in this recipe.

mozzarella cheese with fennel and new potatoes

8 oz. new potatoes, about 12–15

1 fennel bulb

8 oz. mozzarella cheese, drained

½ cup olive oil

¼ cup balsamic vinegar

sea salt and freshly ground black pepper

SERVES 4

Cook the potatoes in a large saucepan of boiling water until just tender, about 12–14 minutes depending on their size. Drain and let cool. When the potatoes are cold, cut them in half and set aside until needed.

Trim the fennel, then cut into halves or quarters. Cut out and discard the hard central core. Using a sharp knife or a mandoline, slice the fennel very finely and set aside.

Slice the mozzarella into thin rounds.

Arrange the potatoes, fennel, and mozzarella in stacks on 4 serving plates, seasoning generously between each layer with salt and pepper.

Sprinkle the stacks with olive oil and balsamic vinegar just before serving.

mozzarella-baked tomatoes

If you can find it, use purple basil, which looks even more spectacular than green. This dish really couldn't be easier, and makes a nice change from roasted tomato halves.

20 ripe tomatoes

8 oz. mozzarella cheese, drained and cut into 20 pieces

½ cup olive oil

a bunch of basil, torn

sea salt and freshly ground black pepper

a large baking tray, lightly oiled

MAKES 20

Cut a deep cross, to about half way down, in the top of each tomato and stuff a piece of mozzarella into each. Transfer to the oiled baking tray and sprinkle with salt and pepper.

Cook in a preheated oven at 325°F for 25 minutes until the tomatoes are beginning to soften and open up. Remove from the oven, sprinkle with oil, and top with basil. Serve warm.

Garlic bread is everybody's favorite snack. Baguette is traditional but any bread works. Try regular white, cottage loaf, ciabatta, Danish split, whole-wheat, mixed grain, or individual rolls and cut them accordingly. For a quick variation, slice the loaf and toast it on one side, then spread the other side with garlic butter and broil.

garlic bread

1 loaf of bread

3 garlic cloves

1 stick unsalted butter, softened

1 teaspoon salt

a bunch of flat-leaf parsley, chopped

freshly ground black pepper

a baking tray

SERVES 4

Cut the bread into slices without cutting the crust all the way through, or cut the loaf in half lengthwise.

Crush the whole cloves of garlic with the flat of a large knife, then peel, chop, and mash to a purée with the salt.

Mix the garlic purée, butter, parsley, and pepper in a bowl, then spread generously on the cut surfaces of the bread.

Wrap the bread in foil, put on a baking tray and cook in a preheated oven at 350°F for 20 minutes. Remove the foil and serve hot.

toasted turkish bread

Harissa paste is a fiery blend of chiles and spices available from Middle Eastern markets, gourmet stores, and some supermarkets. It's great for firing up all sorts of dishes. Stir it into couscous or mix with yogurt and serve as a dip for crudités.

1 teaspoon harissa paste or 1 drop Tabasco

a bunch of cilantro, chopped

2 tablespoons olive oil

¼ cup pitted olives, chopped, about 1½ oz.

2 Anaheim red chiles, seeded and chopped

4 slices small Turkish flatbread, pita bread, or small flour tortillas, separated into disks

a baking tray

SERVES 4

Put the harissa, cilantro, olive oil, olives, and chiles in a small bowl and mix well. Divide the mixture between the pieces of bread, then sandwich the pieces of bread back together.

Put on a baking tray and cook in a preheated oven at 325°F for 10 minutes. Remove and serve hot.

This is such a simple dish that it makes the perfect snack whatever time of day hunger strikes. It tastes amazing, too.

peppered button mushrooms
on buttery toast

4 tablespoons unsalted butter, plus extra for spreading

1 lb. button mushrooms

4 thick slices white bread

sea salt and freshly ground black pepper

SERVES 4

Working in batches if necessary, put the butter in a large skillet, melt over medium heat, add the mushrooms, and sauté until well browned, about 3 minutes. Don't lower the heat too much, or the mushrooms will release all their delicious juices back into the skillet and start to boil, rather than sauté. Season with salt and plenty of black pepper.

Toast the bread until golden brown and spread generously with butter. Put the toast on 4 warm plates and pile the mushrooms on top. Spoon any remaining pan juices over the top, sprinkle with extra pepper, and serve.

zucchini and cheese on toast

Here is a simple combination that tastes like heaven—just make sure that you squeeze the grated zucchini well otherwise it will make the toast soggy. Vegetarian Worcestershire sauce can be bought from health food stores.

2 zucchini, grated

1⅔ cups freshly grated mature Cheddar or Monterey Jack cheese

1 shallot, finely chopped

1 egg, lightly beaten

a dash of Worcestershire sauce

4 slices bread, toasted

sea salt and freshly ground black pepper

SERVES 4

Put the grated zucchini in a clean, dry dishtowel and twist tightly, squeezing out all the excess liquid.

Transfer to a mixing bowl and add the cheese, shallot, egg, Worcestershire sauce, salt, and pepper. Stir thoroughly.

Put the toasted bread on a baking tray, pile the zucchini mixture on top, and cook under a preheated broiler until golden brown. Serve hot.

pan-grilled bruschetta
with red onion marmalade and goat cheese

2 ciabatta rolls,
halved crosswise

4 large handfuls of mixed
salad leaves

1 tablespoon extra virgin olive
oil, plus extra for serving

½ cup soft, mild goat cheese

sea salt and freshly ground
black pepper

RED ONION MARMALADE

2 tablespoons olive oil

1½ lb. red onions, very
thinly sliced

1 bay leaf

1 teaspoon thyme leaves

¼ cup firmly packed
brown sugar

3 tablespoons balsamic
vinegar

⅔ cup red wine

grated zest and juice of
1 unwaxed orange

sea salt and freshly ground
black pepper

SERVES 4

Grilled bread is more than just toast—it stays chewy on the inside and has a smoky flavor and lovely stripes from the grill pan.

First make the red onion marmalade. Heat the oil in a large saucepan until hot. Add the onions, bay leaf, thyme, and salt and black pepper to taste. Cover with a lid and cook over low heat, stirring occasionally, for 30 minutes until the onions are softened and translucent.

Add the sugar, vinegar, red wine, orange zest, and juice. Cook uncovered for a further 1½ hours until no liquid is left and the onions are a dark, rich, red color. Stir frequently during the last 30 minutes to stop the onions from burning.

Let the mixture cool, then transfer to sterilized jars (see page 4). Any leftover marmalade will keep for several weeks in the refrigerator.

Heat a stove-top grill pan until hot. Add the ciabatta and cook for 1–2 minutes on each side until lightly toasted and charred.

Meanwhile, put the salad leaves in a bowl, add the olive oil and salt and pepper to taste. Toss well.

Spread 1 tablespoon of the red onion marmalade on each piece of the toasted ciabatta and put on serving plates. Add a handful of salad leaves and crumble the goat cheese on top. Sprinkle with olive oil and lots of black pepper.

hummus and salad
in turkish flatbread

4 sheets very thin Turkish flatbread

¾ cup hummus

¼ head iceberg lettuce, finely shredded

2 avocados, halved, pitted, and sliced

freshly squeezed juice of 1 lemon

2 tablespoons olive oil

sea salt and freshly ground black pepper

SERVES 4

If Turkish flatbread is hard to find, use pita bread instead—just toast it lightly, open up the pocket, and fill with all the ingredients given here.

Open out the flatbreads and put each one on a piece of wax paper. Spread evenly with the hummus.

Arrange the lettuce on top of the hummus, add the sliced avocado, then sprinkle with the lemon juice and olive oil. Season generously with salt and pepper.

With the help of the wax paper, roll up the bread and filling tightly and shape with your hands into a cylinder, twisting the paper at each end.

Cut the cylinders in half. Eat the wraps within 3 hours of making them for a really good, fresh taste.

Perfect fries should be cooked twice, at two different temperatures—first to cook them through, then in hotter oil to make them crisp and golden.

root vegetable chunky fries
with cilantro mayo

1 lb. sweet potatoes, cut into thick fries

1 lb. potatoes, cut into thick fries

1 lb. parsnips, cut into thick fries

peanut or safflower oil, for frying

sea salt, to serve

CILANTRO MAYO

a large bunch of cilantro, chopped

¼ cup mayonnaise

a squeeze of fresh lime juice

sea salt and freshly ground black pepper

electric deep fryer with fryer basket

SERVES 4

Soak the prepared vegetables in a bowl of cold water for 10 minutes to remove excess starch. Drain and dry well with a clean cloth.

Meanwhile, put the cilantro and mayonnaise in a small food processor, add 1 tablespoon water, and process until blended. Add the lime juice and salt and pepper to taste. Mix well.

Half-fill an electric fryer or large saucepan with oil and heat to about 360°F, or until a cube of bread browns in about 60 seconds. Working in 2–3 batches, plunge the vegetables into the oil and cook for 6–8 minutes, until cooked through but not golden. Remove and drain on paper towels.

Increase the heat to about 385°F, or until a cube of bread browns in 20 seconds. Plunge the fries back into the oil and cook for 2–3 minutes until golden.

Remove, drain on paper towels, and sprinkle with salt. Serve at once with the cilantro mayo.

4 portobello mushrooms, stalks trimmed

1 tablespoon extra virgin olive oil

4 large ciabatta rolls

sea salt and freshly ground black pepper

mixed salad, to serve

CARAMELIZED SHALLOTS

1 tablespoon extra virgin olive oil

1 cup thinly sliced shallots, about 4 oz.

2 tablespoons red currant jelly

1 tablespoon red wine vinegar

salt and freshly ground black pepper

GARLIC MAYONNAISE

1 egg yolk

1 garlic clove, crushed

1 teaspoon freshly squeezed lemon juice

a pinch of salt

⅔ cup light olive oil

SERVES 4

mushroom burgers
with caramelized shallots and garlic mayonnaise

If you have any garlic mayonnaise left over, cover it and put it in the refrigerator—it will keep for up to three days.

First, make the caramelized shallots. Heat the oil in a small skillet, add the shallots, and cook for 15 minutes over low heat without browning. Add the red currant jelly, vinegar, and 1 tablespoon water. Cook for a further 10–15 minutes, until reduced and thickened. Add salt and pepper to taste and let cool.

To make the mayonnaise, put the egg yolk, garlic, lemon juice, and salt in a bowl and beat well. Gradually beat in the oil, a little at a time, until thickened and glossy.

Brush the mushrooms all over with the oil and sprinkle with salt and pepper. Put in a nonstick skillet and cook for 4–5 minutes each side. Cut the ciabatta rolls in half and toast on a preheated stove-top grill pan. Put the mushrooms on 4 of the toasted ciabatta halves and top with the caramelized shallots, some mayonnaise, and the remaining ciabatta halves. Serve with a mixed salad.

grilled artichokes
with chile-lime mayonnaise

Try to find small or baby artichokes for this dish so that they can be cooked straight on the grill without any blanching first. Larger ones will need to be blanched in boiling water for a few minutes then drained before grilling.

18 small artichokes

1 lemon, halved

2 tablespoons extra virgin olive oil

sea salt and freshly ground black pepper

lime wedges, to serve

CHILE-LIME MAYONNAISE

1 dried chipotle chile pepper

2 free-range egg yolks

1¼ cups olive oil

freshly squeezed juice of 1 lime

sea salt

SERVES 6

To make the chile-lime mayonnaise, cover the chipotle with boiling water and let soak for 30 minutes. Drain and pat dry, then cut in half, scrape out the seeds, and discard them.

Finely chop the flesh and put in a food processor. Add the egg yolks and a little salt and blend briefly until frothy. With the blade running, gradually pour the oil through the funnel until the sauce is thick and glossy. Add the lime juice and, if the mayonnaise is too thick, 1 tablespoon warm water. Taste and adjust the seasoning, then cover and set aside.

Trim the stalks from the artichokes and cut off the top 1 inch of the globes. Slice the globes in half lengthwise, and cut out the central "choke" if necessary. Rub the cut surfaces all over with a halved lemon to keep them from discoloring.

Toss the artichokes with the oil and a little salt and pepper. Cook over medium-hot coals for 15–20 minutes, depending on size, until charred and tender, turning halfway through the cooking time. Serve with the chile-lime mayonnaise and wedges of lime.

soups

pasta e fagioli

This hearty soup of pasta and beans is a classic from the region of Puglia in southeast Italy—the pasta shapes traditionally used are orecchiette, meaning "little ears."

2 tablespoons olive oil

1 small onion, finely chopped

2 garlic cloves, finely chopped

1 potato, chopped

2 ripe tomatoes, chopped

5 cups Vegetable Broth (page 233)

a sprig of thyme, sage, or rosemary

2 lb. canned navy beans, about 4 cups, drained and rinsed

8 oz. small dried pasta shapes, such as orecchiette, about 2 cups

a pinch of hot red pepper flakes

sea salt and freshly ground black pepper

freshly grated Parmesan cheese, to serve

SERVES 4

Heat the oil in a large saucepan, add the onion, garlic, and potato, and cook for 3–4 minutes until golden. Add the tomatoes and cook for 2–3 minutes until softened.

Add the broth, herbs, beans, pasta, red pepper flakes, salt, and pepper. Bring to a boil, then simmer for about 10 minutes, until the pasta and potatoes are cooked.

Ladle into 4 bowls and serve sprinkled with a little grated Parmesan.

The color and velvety-smooth flavor of this soup make it a winner with the whole family. Serve with crusty country bread.

butternut and cashew soup

¼ cup olive oil

4 tablespoons unsalted butter

1 onion, chopped

1 butternut squash, about 2 lb., peeled, seeded, and chopped

1 teaspoon medium curry powder

⅔ cup milk

1 cup cashews, chopped

sea salt and freshly ground black pepper

country bread, to serve (optional)

SERVES 4

Heat the olive oil and butter in a large saucepan over medium heat. Add the onion and cook for 5 minutes until soft but not browned.

Add the chopped butternut, curry powder, and a little salt and pepper. Stir, then cook for 5 minutes.

Pour in 2 cups water and the milk, then bring the mixture to a boil, lower the heat, and simmer for 30 minutes.

Add the cashews and cool briefly. Working in batches if necessary, transfer the soup to a blender or food processor and blend until smooth and thick. Alternatively, use a stick blender and blend the soup in the saucepan.

Reheat the soup as necessary. Taste and adjust the seasoning to your liking, then serve hot accompanied by country bread, if using.

green bean and herb broth

¼ cup olive oil

1 onion, very thinly sliced

1 garlic clove, chopped

4 cups Vegetable Broth
(page 233)

8 oz. green beans, cut into
1-inch pieces, about 2 cups

8 oz. runner beans, cut into
1-inch pieces, about 2 cups

8 oz. shelled peas or fava
beans, peeled, about 2 cups

a bunch of chervil, chopped

a bunch of dill, chopped

sea salt and freshly ground
black pepper

SERVES 4

This soup is great served on its own—it makes a perfect light meal. If you need a dish that is a little more filling, add some pasta or noodles at the same time as the broth. The vegetables and herbs in this soup need only quick, light cooking to bring out their delicate flavors.

Heat the olive oil in a large saucepan or Dutch oven. Add the sliced onion and cook over low heat for 10 minutes without letting it brown. Add the garlic and cook gently for a further 5 minutes.

Pour in the broth and add salt and pepper. Bring to a boil, reduce the heat, and simmer for 5 minutes.

Add all the beans to the soup and simmer for 4 minutes, then add the chopped fresh herbs and cook for a further 2 minutes. Serve immediately.

In the cold of the winter, a thick, rich soup is a delight every time—serve it with lots of fresh, warm bread and cold butter. The tarragon drizzle transforms this rather comforting, old-fashioned soup into something stylish and modern!

rich root soup
with green tarragon drizzle

1 tablespoon olive oil

2 onions, chopped

1 garlic clove, chopped

3 celery stalks, chopped, about 1½ cups

1½ cups chopped parsnips, 1 lb.

2½ cups cubed rutabagas, 1 lb.

1½ cups chopped carrots, 1 lb.

1 tablespoon good-quality vegetable bouillon powder

sea salt and freshly ground black pepper

GREEN TARRAGON DRIZZLE

a bunch of tarragon, finely chopped

freshly squeezed juice of ½ lemon

¼ cup olive oil

SERVES 4

Put the oil in a large saucepan, heat gently, then add the onion, garlic, and celery, and cook for 5 minutes without browning. Add the parsnips, rutabagas, and carrots and cook for 3 minutes. Mix the bouillon powder with 1½ quarts boiling water and add to the vegetables. Add salt and pepper to taste, bring to a boil, and simmer for 35 minutes, until the vegetables are tender.

Remove from the heat and let cool slightly. Working in batches if necessary, transfer the soup to a blender or food processor and blend until smooth. Alternatively, use a stick blender and blend in the saucepan.

To make the drizzle, put the tarragon in a bowl and add the lemon juice and oil. Using a stick blender, blend until smooth. Reheat the soup as necessary. Ladle the hot soup into bowls, add a swirl of tarragon drizzle, and serve.

wild mushroom soup
with sour cream and chives

Dried porcini have a gorgeous, intense taste and you only need to add a few to fresh mushrooms to produce a lovely, rich soup. Always rinse porcini well, to remove any dust.

1 oz. dried porcini mushrooms, rinsed thoroughly

4 tablespoons unsalted butter

3 cups sliced portobello mushrooms, 1 lb.

2 garlic cloves, crushed

2 slices white bread, crusts removed

⅔ cup sour cream

a small bunch of chives, chopped

sea salt and freshly ground black pepper

SERVES 4

Put the porcini in a small bowl. Cover with 3 cups boiling water and let soak for 30 minutes.

Meanwhile, put the butter in a large saucepan or wok and heat until melted. Add the sliced mushrooms and cook for about 5 minutes until soft.

Drain the porcini, reserving the soaking liquid. Coarsely chop, then add to the mushrooms in the saucepan or wok. Cook for a further 2 minutes, then add the garlic.

Tear the bread into the pan. Add the reserved porcini soaking liquid and salt and pepper to taste. Bring to a boil, reduce the heat, and simmer for 10 minutes.

Working in batches if necessary, transfer the soup to a blender or food processor and blend until almost smooth. Reheat the soup as necessary. Ladle into bowls and top with a spoonful of sour cream. Sprinkle with chives and freshly ground black pepper, then serve.

rich red bell pepper and bean soup

Canned beans can form the basis of a lot of filling, easy-to-make soups, salads, and entrées, so keep several cans of each kind in your pantry.

2 large red bell peppers, halved, seeded, and cut into ½-inch slices

3 tablespoons olive oil

1 large onion, finely chopped

⅔ cup dry white wine

1½ lb. canned lima beans, about 3 cups, drained and rinsed

3 cups Vegetable Broth (page 233)

4 oz. thin green beans, trimmed, about 1 cup

sea salt and freshly ground black pepper

chile oil or garlic oil, to serve

SERVES 4

Put the bell peppers in a roasting pan, sprinkle with 1 tablespoon olive oil, and some salt and pepper. Transfer to a preheated oven at 400°F and roast for 30 minutes.

Heat the remaining oil in a large saucepan. Add the onion and cook over medium heat for 10 minutes, or until softened and translucent.

Add the wine to the onion and boil for 1 minute. Add the lima beans, broth, and black pepper to taste. Bring to a boil, reduce the heat, and simmer for 15 minutes.

Meanwhile, add the green beans to the bell peppers in the oven and roast for a further 8–10 minutes.

Transfer the lima bean mixture to a blender or food processor and blend until smooth. Reheat the soup as necessary. Ladle into soup plates or bowls, then top with a spoonful of the roasted bell peppers and beans. Sprinkle with the chile or garlic oil and serve.

watercress soup

2 tablespoons olive oil

1 onion, chopped

1 leek, chopped

2 large potatoes, chopped

2 teaspoons all-purpose flour

6 cups Vegetable Broth (page 233)

10 oz. watercress, stalks removed and leaves chopped

a bunch of flat-leaf parsley, chopped

sea salt and freshly ground black pepper

SERVES 8

Watercress has a fresh crunch that releases a subtle peppery taste—a real palate cleanser. Buy it in bunches, with long stems, an abundance of flawless dark green leaves, and a clean fresh smell. Store in the refrigerator, wrapped in damp paper towels, for up to 2 days.

Heat the oil in a large saucepan and add the onion, leek, and potatoes. Cook for 15 minutes until soft and translucent.

Add the flour, mix well, then add the broth and season with salt and pepper. Heat to simmering and cook for 30 minutes.

Using a hand-held stick blender, blend until smooth. Add the watercress and parsley and simmer for 5 minutes. Season with salt and pepper if necessary, then serve.

cheese
and eggs

½ teaspoon cornstarch

1 cup milk

1 lb. Fontina cheese, chopped, about 5 cups

4 tablespoons unsalted butter (optional)

4 egg yolks

freshly ground white pepper

1 white truffle (optional) or truffle oil

TO SERVE

steamed spring vegetables such as baby carrots, baby leeks, baby turnips, asparagus, fennel, and snowpeas, cut into bite-size pieces if necessary

toast or cornbread triangles

a double boiler

SERVES 6

The Italian version of fondue is a speciality of the Valle d'Aosta in the northwest. It is made with Fontina cheese, enriched with egg yolks, then sprinkled decadently with shavings of white truffle from neighboring Piedmont. If you don't have a truffle on hand, a sprinkling of truffle oil will give a hint of the prized fragrance.

fonduta

Put the cornstarch in a small bowl, add 1 tablespoon milk, and stir until dissolved—this is called "slaking."

Put the remaining milk in the top section of a double boiler, then add the cheese and slaked cornstarch. Put over a saucepan of simmering water and heat, stirring constantly, until the cheese melts. Stir in the butter, if using, and remove from the heat.

Put the egg yolks in a bowl and beat lightly. Beat in a few tablespoons of the hot cheese mixture to warm the yolks. Pour this mixture back into the double boiler, stirring vigorously. Return the saucepan to the heat and continue stirring until the mixture thickens.

To serve, ladle the cheese mixture into preheated bowls and sprinkle with freshly ground white pepper and shavings of truffle, if using. Alternatively, sprinkle with a few drops of truffle oil. Serve the bowls surrounded by the prepared vegetables, with toast or cornbread triangles for dipping.

roasted red bell pepper cheese fondue

6 red bell peppers

½ cup dry white wine or tomato juice

2 tablespoons olive oil

6 scallions, finely chopped

3 fresh jalapeño chiles, seeded and finely chopped

¾ cup light cream

4 oz. cream cheese, cut or broken into small pieces, about ½ cup

8 oz. Mexican queso fresco or asadero cheese, crumbled or grated, about 2 cups

1 tablespoon all-purpose flour

TO SERVE

roasted butternut squash sprinkled with paprika

soft tortillas or sourdough bread

quince paste (optional)

a fondue pot

SERVES 6

Roasted red bell peppers have a sweet acidity that blends wonderfully with cheese. This fondue is delicious served over roasted butternut squash sprinkled with paprika.

Roast the bell peppers under a very hot broiler or in the flames of a gas burner, until blackened all over. Transfer to a large bowl and cover with plastic wrap. Let steam for about 10 minutes, then peel off the skin. Halve the peppers and discard the stalks and seeds. Finely slice and reserve one pepper for serving and put the remainder in a food processor. Add the wine or tomato juice and blend to a coarse purée.

Heat the olive oil in a fondue pot and sauté the scallions and jalapeño chiles until soft, about 5–7 minutes. Stir in the pepper purée and simmer for 5 minutes. Stir in the cream and heat but do not boil. Remove the pot from the heat.

Add the cream cheese, stir until melted, and return to the heat. Put the queso fresco or asadero cheese and flour in a bowl, toss well, then gradually add to the fondue, stirring constantly.

Transfer the fondue pot to its tabletop burner and sprinkle with the reserved sliced pepper. Ladle the pepper cheese over the roasted butternut squash and eat with tortillas or sourdough bread. A few slices of quince paste makes an interesting accompaniment.

Vacherin is one of the world's great cheeses. The three varieties are unpasteurized, so they are difficult to find in America. Vacherin Fribourgeois is the one used in cooking. Fontina or raclette cheese are suitable alternatives.

vacherin fondue
with caramelized shallots

2 tablespoons unsalted butter or 2 tablespoons olive oil

12 oz. shallots, thinly sliced, 3 cups

2 teaspoons brown sugar

2 tablespoons balsamic or cider vinegar

2 cups dry white wine

10 oz. Gruyère cheese, grated, about 2 cups

1 tablespoon all-purpose flour

10 oz. Fontina or raclette cheese, grated, about 2 cups

2 tablespoons port wine (optional)

TO SERVE

bread, such as sourdough or baguette, cubed

fresh vegetables, for dipping

SERVES 6

Put the butter or oil in a cheese fondue pot or large saucepan and melt over medium heat. Add the shallots, reduce the heat to low, and cook for 10 minutes. Stir in the sugar, then the vinegar, and cook for a further 10 minutes. Remove a few shallots and set aside for serving.

Pour in the wine, bring to a boil, then reduce to a simmer.

Put the Gruyère and flour in a bowl and toss well. Gradually add the cheese to the simmering fondue mixture, stirring constantly. Stir in the Fontina or raclette, followed by the port, if using.

Transfer the fondue pot to its tabletop burner, add the reserved shallots, and serve the fondue with cubes of bread and vegetables for dipping. Alternatively, put a few slices of baguette in 6 bowls and ladle the fondue over the top.

creamy scrambled eggs
with goat cheese

12 free-range eggs

½ cup light cream

2 tablespoons chopped
fresh marjoram or thyme

4 tablespoons unsalted butter

8 oz. goat cheese, chopped,
about 1 cup

a handful of nasturtium
flowers, torn (optional)

sea salt and cracked black
pepper

4 slices of toasted walnut
bread, to serve

SERVES 4

Stirring a little creamy goat cheese into lightly scrambled eggs transforms a simple dish into a delicious light lunch. The nasturtium flowers are optional, but they do add a delightful flash of color as well as a delicate, peppery flavor.

Put the eggs in a bowl and beat in the cream, marjoram or thyme, and a little salt and pepper. Melt the butter in a nonstick saucepan, add the eggs, and stir over low heat until the eggs are just beginning to set.

Stir in the goat cheese and continue to cook briefly, still stirring, until the cheese melts into the eggs. Add the nasturtium flowers, if using, and spoon onto the 4 slices of toast. Serve immediately.

arugula eggs with salsa verde

4 free-range eggs

1 teaspoon unsalted butter

1 cup sliced arugula

salt and freshly ground black pepper

ARUGULA SALSA VERDE

2 cups chopped arugula

½ bunch chives, chopped

¼ cup extra virgin olive oil

sea salt and freshly ground black pepper

TO SERVE

1 cup mixed salad leaves

½ cup walnuts, broken into pieces

shavings of fresh Parmesan cheese

SERVES 2

An omelet-style dish that is fast to cook—have the ingredients ready before you start. To serve four people, double the ingredients, but make the eggs in two batches.

To make the arugula salsa verde, put the arugula in a blender or food processor, add the chives, olive oil, and 2 tablespoons water. Blend until smooth. Add salt and pepper to taste. Set aside.

Crack the eggs into a small bowl and beat briefly. Season with salt and pepper to taste.

Heat the butter in a wok or skillet until foaming. Add the 1 cup of arugula and cook, stirring, for about 30 seconds.

Add the eggs and gently swirl around the surface of the wok. Cook until golden brown underneath, but still slightly soft and runny on the top.

Meanwhile, divide the salad between 2 plates and sprinkle with the walnuts. Using 2 wooden spoons, cut the omelet into 4 pieces and put on top of the salad. Top with Parmesan shavings and serve at once with the salsa verde.

With its lovely, earthy flavors, a frittata is an Italian version of the Spanish tortilla or the French omelet. Different ingredients are added depending on the region or the season.

mixed mushroom frittata

3 tablespoons extra virgin olive oil

2 shallots, finely chopped

2 garlic cloves, finely chopped

1 tablespoon chopped fresh thyme leaves

3 cups mixed wild and cultivated mushrooms, such as chanterelle, portobello, shiitake, and white button mushrooms

6 eggs

2 tablespoons chopped fresh flat-leaf parsley

sea salt and freshly ground black pepper

SERVES 6

Put 2 tablespoons oil in a nonstick skillet, heat gently, then add the shallots, garlic, and thyme. Sauté gently for 5 minutes until softened but not browned.

Meanwhile, brush off any dirt clinging to the mushrooms and wipe the caps. Chop or slice coarsely and add to the skillet. Sauté for 4–5 minutes until just starting to release their juices. Remove from the heat.

Put the eggs in a bowl with the parsley and a little salt and pepper, and beat briefly. Add the mushroom mixture to the eggs and stir. Wipe the skillet clean.

Heat the remaining tablespoon of oil in the clean skillet and pour in the egg and mushroom mixture. Cook over medium heat for 8–10 minutes until set on the bottom. Transfer the skillet to a preheated broiler and cook for 2–3 minutes until the top is set and spotted brown. Let cool and serve at room temperature.

salads
and sides

You can make this salad on a grill or in a stove-top grill pan, or by roasting the vegetables in the oven. Take your pick.

asparagus and roasted bell peppers

3 red bell peppers

2 red onions

1 lb. asparagus, trimmed

⅓ cup olive oil

2 tablespoons balsamic vinegar

sea salt and freshly ground black pepper

2 oz. Parmesan cheese, cut into shavings, to serve (optional)

SERVES 4

Cut the bell pepper flesh away from the core in flat pieces to make grilling easier. Put the pepper pieces skin-side down on a preheated stove-top grill pan and cook until the skin is blistered and turning black.

Transfer the peppers to a small bowl and cover the bowl with plastic wrap—let steam for 10 minutes. When cool enough to handle, peel the skins away from the flesh.

Cut the onions into wedges, leaving the root end intact to hold them together. Add to the grill pan and cook for 4 minutes on each side, then add the asparagus to the grill pan and cook for about 3 minutes or until just soft.

Put the peppers in a bowl with the onions, asparagus, olive oil, vinegar, salt, and pepper. Toss to coat, then serve warm or at room temperature with shavings of Parmesan, if using.

1 tablespoon sugar

1 tablespoon balsamic vinegar

1 tablespoon cider vinegar

2 inches fresh ginger, peeled
and finely grated

freshly squeezed juice of
½ lemon

3 tablespoons extra virgin
olive oil

1 small red onion, halved and
sliced lengthwise

4 golden beets, cooked
and peeled

a bundle of small mushrooms,
such as Japanese hon shimeji
or shiitakes

1 garlic clove, finely chopped

sea salt and freshly ground
black pepper

SERVES 4

Hon shimeji mushrooms grow in clumps like families—tiny babies sprout at the feet of the parents. To keep the silkiness of their satin-like flesh, they need a short flying visit to a hot skillet. If they are unavailable, use sliced shiitakes or regular mushrooms instead. Here golden beets have been used rather than the regular purple ones.

baby mushroom salad
with golden beets and ginger

Put the sugar, balsamic, and cider vinegar in a bowl and stir until the sugar dissolves. Take the grated ginger in your hand and squeeze the juice into the bowl. Discard the gratings. Add the lemon juice and 2 tablespoons olive oil and beat well. Add the onion.

Cut the beets into small wedges, add to the bowl, sprinkle with salt and pepper, and mix. Set aside for at least 30 minutes to let the beets absorb the flavors of the dressing.

Just before serving, put the remaining 1 tablespoon olive oil in a skillet, heat well, add the mushrooms and garlic, and cook over high heat until seared but not soft. Add to the bowl and toss in the dressing.

Divide the vegetables and dressing between 4 bowls and serve.

new potato salad
with gazpacho dressing

1 lb. baby new potatoes,
scrubbed but not peeled

GAZPACHO DRESSING

2 large, ripe tomatoes, halved,
seeded, and chopped

2 oz. roasted red bell peppers
(from a jar), chopped,
about ¼ cup

½ small red onion, chopped

1 garlic clove, chopped

3 tablespoons extra virgin
olive oil

2 teaspoons red wine vinegar

a pinch of sugar

a bunch of flat-leaf parsley,
chopped

sea salt and freshly ground
black pepper

SERVES 4

Gazpacho is the famous Spanish chilled soup, made with tomatoes, bell peppers, onions, and garlic. Use the same ingredients to make a fresh dressing for this simple salad of new potatoes. Add the dressing to the potatoes while they are hot, even if you aren't eating them right away, as this will help the flavors to infuse.

Bring a large saucepan of lightly salted water to a boil, add the potatoes, and return to a boil. Reduce the heat and simmer for about 12 minutes or until the potatoes are just tender when pierced with a knife.

Meanwhile, put the dressing ingredients in a large bowl and mix well. Add plenty of salt and freshly ground pepper.

Drain the potatoes thoroughly and empty them into the dressing. Mix well and serve hot or at room temperature.

1½ lb. butternut squash, peeled, seeded, and chopped

1 tablespoon extra virgin olive oil

1 tablespoon chopped fresh thyme leaves

1 lb. dried penne, or similar pasta

8 oz. feta cheese, chopped

8 oz. cherry tomatoes, about 2 cups, halved

¼ cup chopped fresh basil

¼ cup pumpkin seeds, toasted in a dry skillet

sea salt and freshly ground black pepper

DRESSING

½ cup extra virgin olive oil

3 tablespoons tapenade

freshly squeezed juice of 1 lemon

1 teaspoon clear honey

sea salt and freshly ground black pepper

SERVES 6

Ready-made tapenade is available in supermarkets and gourmet stores. Some stores make their own and these are definitely worth seeking out for this dish.

pasta, squash, and feta salad
with olive dressing

Put the butternut squash in a bowl or plastic bag, then add the oil, thyme, salt, and pepper. Toss well, then arrange in a single layer in a roasting pan. Roast in a preheated oven at 400°F for about 25 minutes, or until golden and tender. Let cool.

To make the dressing, put the olive oil, tapenade, lemon juice, and honey in a bowl. Beat well, then add salt and pepper to taste.

Bring a large saucepan of lightly salted water to a boil, add the pasta, and cook for about 10 minutes until *al dente* (just cooked but still slightly firm in the middle). Drain well, then immediately stir in ¼ cup of the dressing. Let cool.

When cool, put the pasta and squash in a salad bowl, mix gently, then add the feta cheese, cherry tomatoes, basil, and toasted pumpkin seeds. Just before serving, stir in the remaining dressing.

Wintry, festive sumptuousness, thanks to the deep
red of the beets and the bright white of the cheese.

beet, goat cheese, and pine nut salad
with melba toast

1½ lb. small, unpeeled beets, trimmed

12 slices white sliced bread

1 lb. mixed leaves

8 oz. crumbly goat cheese

4 oz. pine nuts, 1 cup, toasted in a dry skillet

a bunch of basil

2 garlic cloves, chopped

½ cup olive oil

freshly squeezed juice of 2 lemons

sea salt and freshly ground black pepper

SERVES 12

Put the beets in a roasting pan and roast in a preheated oven at 350°F for 45 minutes. Remove the beets from the oven, let cool, then peel and quarter them.

Meanwhile, to make the Melba toast, toast the slices of bread, then remove the crusts. Using a large, sharp knife, split each piece of toast through the middle, to give 2 whole slices of toast with 1 soft bread side each. Cut in half diagonally, then cook under a preheated broiler, soft side up, until golden and curled. Watch the toasts carefully, as they can burn quickly.

Put the mixed leaves on a big serving dish, add the beets, crumble the goat cheese on top, then sprinkle with pine nuts and torn basil leaves.

Put the garlic, oil, and lemon juice in a small bowl or jar. Add salt and pepper, mix well, then pour over the salad. Serve with the Melba toast.

2 eggplant, about 8 inches, sliced diagonally into 1-inch slices

¼ cup olive oil

grated zest of 1 unwaxed lemon

2 tablespoons thyme leaves

freshly ground black pepper

FETA SALAD

24 black olives, pitted and chopped

1 small red onion, chopped

½ cucumber, chopped

2 tomatoes, chopped, about 3 cups

⅓ cup feta cheese, crumbled, 3 oz.

a bunch of flat-leaf parsley, chopped

3 tablespoons olive oil

1 small garlic clove, crushed

freshly squeezed juice of ½ lemon

sea salt and freshly ground black pepper

SERVES 4

eggplant steaks with feta salad

The feta salad adds a lovely touch of summer freshness to this dish. This can be served as a meal in itself, or as an accompaniment to other grilled dishes.

Put the eggplant slices, oil, lemon zest, and thyme in a bowl. Toss to coat and add black pepper to taste. Set aside.

To make the feta salad, put the olives, onion, cucumber, tomatoes, feta, parsley, oil, and garlic in a second bowl and mix gently. Set aside.

Cook the eggplant slices on a preheated grill or grill pan or under a medium broiler for about 5 minutes on each side until lightly barred with lines and very soft. Sprinkle the salad with lemon juice, salt, and pepper to taste. Divide the eggplant and salad between 4 plates and serve.

4 slices country bread, cubed

4 ripe tomatoes, cut into wedges

6 inches cucumber, peeled and cut into chunks

1 red onion, sliced

a bunch of flat-leaf parsley, coarsely chopped

⅔ cup olives, pitted

2 tablespoons capers, rinsed and drained

¼ cup olive oil

1½ tablespoons wine vinegar

freshly squeezed juice of ½ lemon

1 teaspoon sugar

sea salt and freshly ground black pepper

SERVES 4

This Tuscan salad, better made with day-old bread, is the perfect way to use up leftovers. It is very flexible, so use whatever ingredients you have on hand—sourdough bread, a little garlic, a bunch of basil.

panzanella

Put the cubed bread in a large bowl with the tomato, cucumber, onion, and chopped parsley.

Add the olives, capers, olive oil, vinegar, lemon juice, sugar, salt, and pepper, then mix well.

Let the salad stand for 1 hour before serving so the bread soaks up the juices and all the flavors mingle.

summer leaf
and herb salad

inner leaves from 2 large
romaine lettuce hearts

8 oz. mixed salad leaves, such
as radicchio, mâche (lamb's
lettuce or corn salad), mizuna,
or endive

a handful of mixed, fresh,
soft-leaf herbs such as basil,
chives, dill, and mint

HONEY LEMON DRESSING

1 garlic clove, crushed

½ cup extra virgin olive oil

1 tablespoon freshly squeezed
lemon juice

1 teaspoon honey

1 teaspoon Dijon mustard

sea salt and freshly ground
black pepper

SERVES 4

There are thousands of recipes for simple leaf salads, so what makes one better than the next? I think it's just a matter of taste, and this version is one of my favorites.

Put the dressing ingredients in a bowl or small jug and set aside to infuse for at least 1 hour. Just before serving, strain out the garlic.

Wash the salad leaves, spin dry in a salad spinner (or pat dry with paper towels), and transfer to a plastic bag. Chill for 30 minutes to make the leaves crisp.

Put the leaves and herbs in a large salad bowl, add a little of the dressing, and toss well to coat evenly. Add a little more dressing to taste, then serve.

summer beans and couscous salad

1 cup couscous, 6 oz.

4 oz. chopped green beans, about 1 cup

4 oz. shelled and peeled fava beans, chopped, about 1 cup (optional)

4 oz. shelled green peas, fresh or frozen, about 1 cup

4 oz. sugar snap peas, trimmed, about 1 cup

grated zest and juice of 2 unwaxed lemons

⅓ cup olive oil

2 teaspoons Spanish sweet paprika

1 garlic clove, chopped

sea salt

SERVES 4

A great, fresh summer dish. It's full of fresh flavors and looks bright and colorful.

Put the couscous in a bowl, cover with boiling water, mix well, cover, and let stand for 10 minutes until swollen.

Bring a large saucepan of water to a boil, then add the green beans and fava beans, if using, and cook for 5 minutes. Add the green peas and sugar snap peas and cook for a further 3 minutes. Drain and refresh under cold running water until the vegetables are cold (otherwise they will lose their bright fresh color).

Drain the couscous. Transfer to a large bowl and add the beans and peas, lemon zest and juice, olive oil, paprika, garlic, and salt. Mix well, then serve.

tomato tapenade salad

1 small focaccia loaf, torn into bite-size pieces

8 large tomatoes, each chopped into 8 pieces

20 kalamata olives, squashed and pitted

2 tablespoons baby capers, rinsed and drained

1 garlic clove, chopped

2 tablespoons extra virgin olive oil

½ teaspoon salt

a pinch of sugar

freshly ground black pepper

TO SERVE

a bunch of basil leaves, torn

extra virgin olive oil

a baking tray

SERVES 4

In Provence, a tapenade is a paste of anchovies, capers, and olives, but I've used just capers and olives as the basis for this salad. Use the ripest red tomatoes, so there are plenty of lovely juices to soak up with the toasted focaccia.

Put the focaccia pieces on a baking tray. Put in a preheated oven at 425°F and bake for 12–15 minutes until golden.

Meanwhile, put the tomatoes in a large bowl. Add the olives, capers, garlic, oil, salt, sugar, and black pepper and mix.

Divide the toasted focaccia pieces between 4 large serving plates and top with a large spoonful of the tomato mixture. Sprinkle with basil and oil, then serve.

This is a great summer salad. The combination of beans and fresh mint is very refreshing and clean on the palate. To turn this salad into an entrée, add some crumbled feta cheese or sliced hard-cooked eggs.

bean and mint salad

4 oz. fava beans, shelled and peeled, about 1 cup (optional)

8 oz. shelled green peas, fresh or frozen, about 2 cups

8 oz. green beans, trimmed, about 2 cups

8 scallions, trimmed and sliced

a large bunch of mint, chopped

3 tablespoons olive oil

grated zest and juice of 1 unwaxed lemon

sea salt and freshly ground black pepper

SERVES 4

Bring a large saucepan of water to a boil, add the fava beans, if using, and cook for 5 minutes. Add the peas and green beans and continue cooking for 3 minutes. Drain, cool quickly under cold running water, then drain thoroughly.

Put the scallions and mint in a large bowl. Add the beans, then sprinkle with the olive oil, lemon zest and juice, salt, and pepper. Toss well and serve.

herby potato rösti

Sautéing creates the lovely crispy crust that's essential for rösti. They are delicious served as an accompaniment or simply served with a green salad.

3 large potatoes, peeled

3–4 large sage leaves

a sprig of thyme, leaves stripped

¼ cup olive oil

sea salt and freshly ground black pepper

SERVES 6

Grate the potatoes on the coarse side of a box grater and dry well on paper towels. Put the grated potato in a bowl.

Finely chop the sage and thyme leaves, discarding any woody stalks. Add the herbs to the grated potato and mix well.

Using your hands, shape a heaped tablespoon of the mixture into a ball. Shape 2 more potato balls in the same way.

Heat half the oil in a large skillet until hot. Add the shaped potato cakes to the skillet and flatten with a spatula. Sauté for 5 minutes until golden.

Turn the rösti over and lower the heat. Continue to cook for 5–10 minutes until golden and cooked through. Transfer to a very low oven to keep them warm. Repeat with the remaining mixture.

Transfer the rösti to a serving plate, sprinkle with salt and pepper, and serve immediately.

This is a flavorsome, yet simple alternative to boiled carrots. Sweet and buttery, it is perfect comfort food.

carrot and spinach
butter mash

1 lb. carrots, peeled and chopped

6 tablespoons butter

8 oz. spinach, chopped, about 2 cups

sea salt and freshly ground black pepper

SERVES 8

Cook the carrots in a saucepan of lightly salted boiling water for about 20 minutes, or until tender. Drain well.

Return the carrots to the pan and put over low heat. Steam off the excess water, stirring frequently, for 2 minutes.

Remove the pan from the heat, add the butter, salt, and pepper, and mash the carrots well. Add the spinach to the mash and stir for 2 minutes, until wilted. Serve immediately.

pizzas, savory tarts, and breads

A robust pizza packed with plenty of Italian flavors. To enjoy this at its best, eat it the moment it comes out of the oven, while the cheese is still bubbling.

charred vegetable cornmeal pizza

1 medium zucchini, thickly sliced

1 small eggplant, cubed

4 plum tomatoes, halved

8 unpeeled garlic cloves

1 red onion, cut into wedges

a few sprigs of thyme

2 tablespoons olive oil

1 quantity Cornmeal Pizza Dough (page 226)

flour, for dusting

8 oz. dolcelatte cheese, chopped

sea salt and freshly ground black pepper

a handful of fresh basil leaves, to serve

a pizza stone or large baking tray

SERVES 4

Preheat the oven to 425°F and put a pizza stone or baking tray in the oven.

Put the zucchini, eggplant, tomatoes, garlic, red onion, and thyme in a roasting pan. Add salt and pepper and sprinkle with the oil. Cook for 30 minutes, stirring from time to time, until softened and a little charred.

Lower the oven temperature to 400°F. Roll out the dough on a lightly floured surface to 12-inch diameter and spoon the vegetables over the top.

Carefully transfer the dough to the hot pizza stone or baking tray and cook for 15 minutes. Remove the pizza from the oven and top with the dolcelatte. Return to the oven and cook for a further 5–10 minutes, until crisp and golden.

Sprinkle with the basil leaves, cut into wedges, and serve hot.

The herby, zingy gremolata is wonderful with the creamy melted cheese—quite a change from your everyday pizza-parlor calzone.

molten cheese and gremolata calzone

2 garlic cloves, crushed

½ cup finely chopped fresh
flat-leaf parsley

grated zest of 1 unwaxed
lemon

1 tablespoon olive oil

1 lb. Taleggio, Brie, or
Camembert cheese

double quantity Pizza Dough
(page 226)

flour, for dusting

sea salt and freshly ground
black pepper

a pizza stone or large baking tray

SERVES 6

Preheat the oven to 400°F and put a pizza stone or baking tray in the oven.

To make the gremolata, put the garlic, parsley, lemon zest, and oil in a bowl. Add salt and pepper to taste and mix well.

Divide the dough into 6 equal pieces. Put on a lightly floured surface and roll each piece into an oval about 10 inches long. Cut the cheese into 6 even slices or wedges and put a slice on one half of each dough oval. Spoon the gremolata over the cheese. Dampen the edges of the dough and fold the dough over to enclose the filling. Press the edges together firmly to seal. Dust with a little flour.

Transfer to the hot pizza stone or baking tray and bake for 20–25 minutes, until crisp and golden. Serve hot.

Spinach and egg pizzas are a favorite in pizza restaurants everywhere, and you can easily make them at home. It doesn't matter if the yolk is a bit hard, but make sure it goes onto the pizza whole.

fiorentina

12 oz. young spinach leaves, 3 cups

1 tablespoon unsalted butter

2 garlic cloves, crushed

1 quantity Pizza Dough (page 226)

1–2 tablespoons olive oil

1 cup Tomato Sauce (pages 228–229)

8 oz. mozzarella cheese, drained and thinly sliced, 1 cup

4 free-range eggs

½ cup finely grated fontina or Gruyère cheese, 4 oz.

sea salt and freshly ground black pepper

a pizza stone or large baking tray

SERVES 4

Preheat the oven to 425°F and put a pizza stone or baking tray in the oven.

Wash the spinach thoroughly and put in a large saucepan. Cover with a lid and cook for 2–3 minutes, until the spinach wilts. Drain well and, when the spinach is cool enough to handle, squeeze out any excess water with your hands.

Melt the butter in a skillet and cook the garlic for 1 minute. Add the drained spinach and cook for a further 3–4 minutes. Add salt and pepper to taste.

Divide the dough into 4. Put on a lightly floured surface and roll out each piece to about 7 inches diameter. Brush with a little oil and spoon the tomato sauce on top. Put the spinach on the bases, leaving a space in the middle for the egg. Put the mozzarella on top of the spinach, sprinkle with a little more oil, salt, and plenty of black pepper.

Carefully transfer to the hot pizza stone or baking tray and cook for 10 minutes. Remove from the oven and crack an egg in the middle of each pizza. Top with the fontina or Gruyère and return to the oven for a further 5–10 minutes, until the base is crisp and golden, and the eggs have just set. Serve immediately.

What is it about caramelized onions? They smell divine, especially when cooked in butter. These simple onion tarts, topped with creamy goat cheese, are best served warm, although they are also good cold.

onion, thyme, and goat cheese tarts

4 tablespoons unsalted butter

2 cups thinly sliced onions, 1 lb.

2 garlic cloves, crushed

1 tablespoon chopped fresh thyme leaves

12 oz. puff pastry dough, defrosted if frozen

flour, for dusting

8 oz. log goat cheese

sea salt and freshly ground black pepper

a baking tray

MAKES 8

Put the butter in a skillet, melt over low heat, then add the onions, garlic, and thyme, and sauté gently for 20–25 minutes, until softened and golden. Season with salt and pepper and let cool.

Put the pastry dough on a lightly floured surface and roll out to form a rectangle, 8 x 16 inches, trimming the edges. Cut the rectangle in half lengthwise and into 4 crosswise, making 8 pieces about 4 inches square.

Divide the onion mixture between the squares, spreading it over the top, leaving a thin border around the edges. Cut the cheese into 8 slices and arrange in the center of each square.

Transfer the squares to a large baking tray and bake in a preheated oven at 425°F for about 12–15 minutes until the dough has risen and the cheese is golden. Let cool a little, then serve warm.

artichoke and cheese tart

This flexible and remarkably easy tart can be topped with all sorts of vegetables and any of your favorite cheeses—the combinations are limitless, so don't hesitate to experiment.

8 oz. puff pastry dough, defrosted if frozen

5 pieces roasted bell pepper in oil, drained and cut into 1-inch strips

1 lb. canned artichoke hearts in oil, drained

3 onions, sliced

8 oz. baby leeks, trimmed

8 oz. cheese, coarsely grated or crumbled, 2 cups

1 egg yolk, beaten

2 tablespoons extra virgin olive oil

sea salt and freshly ground black pepper

a baking tray, lightly oiled

SERVES 10

Preheat the oven to 425°F. Roll out the pastry dough to a rectangle measuring 12 x 7 inches and place on a damp baking tray. Prick all over with a fork, then bake in the preheated oven for 20 minutes.

Put the roasted bell peppers in a large bowl with the artichokes, onions, leeks, cheese, salt, and pepper. Mix well.

Remove the cooked tart crust from the oven, then brush all over with a little egg yolk.

Spread out the filling evenly on the crust. Return to the oven and bake for a further 30 minutes.

Serve hot or at room temperature, lightly sprinkled with a little extra virgin olive oil.

wild mushroom and potato pasties
with parmesan and truffle oil

2 large baking potatoes, unpeeled

6 tablespoons unsalted butter, melted

4 fresh porcini mushrooms, sliced, or 2 handfuls of other wild mushrooms or 4 cremini, sliced

2 garlic cloves, finely chopped

2 sprigs of thyme or flat-leaf parsley, chopped, or 2 teaspoons chopped rosemary leaves

2 boxes pie crust mix, 9 oz. each

flour, for dusting

1–2 teaspoons truffle oil

shavings of fresh Parmesan cheese

1 egg, lightly beaten, to glaze

sea salt and freshly ground black pepper

salad leaves, to serve

a baking tray, lightly oiled

SERVES 4

This is where a little bottle of truffle oil will give extra mushroom flavor and a bit of glamour. Mushrooms, especially wild ones, are natural partners with butter, cheese, potato, and truffle oil.

Put the potatoes in a saucepan, cover with cold water, bring to a boil, and cook until half-done (test with the point of a knife). Drain. Holding the hot potatoes in a dishtowel, peel off the skins, then cut into thick slices.

Put 2½ tablespoons of the butter in a skillet, heat until foaming, add the mushrooms, salt, and pepper, and sauté over high heat until beginning to brown on both sides. Add the garlic and herbs, stir-fry for a few seconds, then remove from the heat and let cool.

Make the pie crust dough according to the instructions on the package, then put on a floured work surface and roll out to about ⅛ inch thick. Cut into 2 rectangles. Put the potatoes and mushrooms in layers in the middle of each rectangle, sprinkling each layer with truffle oil, shavings of Parmesan, the remaining melted butter, salt, and pepper.

Fold in the long edges of the dough rectangles to contain the filling and make an overlapping join on top. Turn the package over and put on the greased baking tray. Make 3 parallel diagonal cuts in the tops, brush with the beaten egg, then bake in a preheated oven at 375°F for about 30 minutes until golden. Cut the packages diagonally into triangles and serve with salad leaves.

There is nothing more satisfying to bake, or to eat, than homemade bread. This Italian loaf, here spiked with rosemary and cherry tomatoes is an ideal accompaniment to an Italian soup, such as the Pasta e Fagioli soup on page 62.

focaccia

3 cups bread flour, plus extra for dusting

1 package (¼ oz.) active dry yeast

½ cup extra virgin olive oil, plus extra for greasing and brushing

12 cherry tomatoes

leaves from a sprig of rosemary

coarse sea salt

a baking tray, lightly oiled

SERVES 6

Put the flour and yeast in a food processor. With the motor on low speed, gradually add the oil and 1¼ cups warm water until the mixture forms a soft dough. Remove to a lightly floured surface and knead for 5 minutes.

Transfer to the prepared baking tray and, using your hands, spread it evenly to the edges. Brush all over with oil, push the cherry tomatoes and rosemary leaves lightly into the surface of the dough at regular intervals, and sprinkle with sea salt.

Cover with a damp, clean dishtowel and put in a warm place for 40 minutes until doubled in size.

Preheat the oven to 400°F and bake for 20 minutes, until golden. Serve warm or at room temperature.

soda bread

In the past, country people worked hard and the traditional way to top up their energy levels was with a substantial meal at dinner. Served with a good, flavorful cheese, this lovely bread provides the perfect boost.

3⅓ cups whole-wheat flour

1 teaspoon baking soda

1 teaspoon cream of tartar

a pinch of salt

2 tablespoons unsalted butter, cut into small cubes

1¼ cups milk

flour, for dusting

TO SERVE

sharp cheese, sliced

unsalted butter

jelly

a baking tray, lightly floured

MAKES 1 LOAF

Sift the flour, baking soda, cream of tartar, and salt in a large bowl. Rub the butter into the flour with your fingertips. Make a well in the center. Pour in the milk and mix with a round-bladed knife to give a soft dough.

Transfer the dough to a lightly floured surface and knead until smooth, about 4 minutes. Shape the dough into a round loaf 6 inches diameter and flatten the top slightly. Place on the baking tray and use a sharp knife to score a cross about ½ inch deep in the top of the dough, making quarters.

Bake in a preheated oven at 350°F for 35 minutes. Remove from the oven and, protecting your hands with a dishtowel, tap the bottom of the loaf with your knuckles—when cooked, it should sound hollow; if it doesn't, bake for a few minutes more.

Serve warm, topped with slices of sharp cheese or spread with butter and jelly.

pasta
and noodles

This dish can be rustled up in a matter of minutes. All you need is fresh broccoli and a few basic ingredients.

broccoli and pine nut pesto pasta

6 oz. dried penne or similar pasta, about 3 cups

8 oz. broccoli, cut into florets

2 tablespoons pine nuts

3 tablespoons olive oil

3 garlic cloves, finely chopped

1 chile, such as serrano, seeded and finely chopped

½ lemon

sea salt and freshly ground black pepper

shavings of fresh Parmesan cheese, to serve

SERVES 2

Bring a large saucepan of water to a boil. Add a pinch of salt, then the pasta, and cook until *al dente*, according to the timings on the package.

Cook the broccoli in a separate saucepan of lightly salted boiling water for about 12 minutes until very soft. Meanwhile, heat a dry skillet until hot, add the pine nuts, and cook, turning them often, for 3–4 minutes, until golden and toasted. Remove to a plate and set aside.

Heat the olive oil in a small saucepan and add the garlic and chile. Gently cook for 2–3 minutes until softened. Remove from the heat and set aside.

Drain the broccoli, return it to the pan, and mash coarsely with a fork.

Drain the pasta and return it to the warm pan. Add the mashed broccoli, garlic and chile oil, and toasted pine nuts. Mix well, squeeze in a little lemon juice, and add salt and pepper to taste.

Divide between 2 serving bowls and top with fresh Parmesan shavings. Sprinkle with pepper and serve.

This isn't an ordinary baked lasagne: rather it is a regular pasta dish, using lasagne sheets dressed with layers of rosemary-scented porcini under blankets of soft cheese. No baking. Of course you can use other mushrooms instead of porcini, just don't use dried porcini.

autumn lasagne with soft goat cheese

3 tablespoons unsalted butter

1 tablespoon olive oil

4 large fresh porcini, or other wild mushrooms or portobellos, sliced

leaves from a sprig of rosemary

16 sheets fresh lasagne

3 free-range egg yolks

3 tablespoons heavy cream

8 oz. soft, mild goat cheese or fresh ricotta, about 1 cup

shavings of fresh Parmesan cheese

sea salt and freshly ground black pepper

SERVES 4

Put the butter and olive oil in a skillet and heat until foaming. Add the sliced porcini and rosemary leaves and sauté until browned on both sides. Remove from the heat and keep the mushrooms warm.

Bring a large saucepan of salted water to a boil, add the lasagne sheets, and cook, stirring gently from time to time to keep the sheets separate, until *al dente*, according to the timings on the package.

Put the egg yolks, cream, salt, and pepper in a large heatproof bowl set over a saucepan of simmering water. Beat with a balloon whisk until the mixture is heated through, about 4 minutes. Drain the lasagne, draping the sheets around the rim of a colander, then add to the bowl of egg mixture and toss carefully. (You have 16 sheets, to allow for breakages.)

To assemble, put a folded sheet of dressed lasagne on each warm plate. Add a small spoonful of goat cheese, some shavings of Parmesan, and 2 slices of porcini to each serving. Repeat the layers, then top with a sheet of lasagne and extra shavings of Parmesan. Spoon the remaining eggy cream over the top and serve.

A simplified version of that old-time favorite, macaroni and cheese, but with no flour and no risk of lumps.

three cheese baked penne

12 oz. dried penne or similar pasta, about 6 cups

2 cups mascarpone cheese, 1 lb.

2 tablespoons whole-grain mustard

10 oz. Fontina cheese, grated, 3 cups

¼ cup freshly grated Parmesan cheese

sea salt and freshly ground black pepper

a baking dish, about 12 x 8 inches

SERVES 4

Bring a large saucepan of water to a boil. Add a pinch of salt, then the pasta, and cook until *al dente*, according to the timings on the package.

Drain the pasta well and return it to the warm pan. Add the mascarpone and mix. Add the mustard, Fontina, and Parmesan, with salt and pepper to taste. Mix.

Transfer to the pasta mixture to the baking dish and cook in a preheated oven at 400°F for 25–30 minutes until golden and bubbling.

pasta with roasted pumpkin
and sage, lemon, and mozzarella butter

Tantalizing pockets of melting garlic butter flavored with herbs and cheese complement the succulent chunks of roast pumpkin. The flavored butter is also brilliant for making garlic bread—it melts between the slices of bread to a deliciously moist and stretchy filling.

2 tablespoons olive oil

1 lb. pumpkin or butternut squash

1 teaspoon cumin seeds

6 oz. fresh mozzarella cheese, drained and chopped

4 tablespoons unsalted butter, softened

2 garlic cloves, crushed

2 teaspoons chopped fresh sage leaves, plus extra whole leaves, to serve

grated zest and juice of 1 unwaxed lemon

10 oz. dried pasta, such as fusilli bucati or cavatappi, about 5 cups

sea salt and freshly ground black pepper

SERVES 4

Put the olive oil in a roasting pan and transfer to the oven for 5 minutes, until hot.

Using a small, sharp knife, peel the pumpkin or squash, remove the seeds, and cut the flesh into cubes, about 1 inch.

Add the cumin seeds to the hot oil in the roasting pan, then add the pumpkin or squash and salt and pepper to taste. Toss to coat. Roast in a preheated oven at 400°F for 30 minutes, turning the pumpkin or squash from time to time until tender and golden.

Put the mozzarella, butter, garlic, sage, lemon zest and juice, salt, and pepper in a food processor. Work into a coarse paste. Transfer to a sheet of wax paper and roll into a cylinder. Chill for at least 20 minutes or until firm enough to slice.

Meanwhile, bring a large saucepan of water to a boil. Add a good pinch of salt, then the pasta, and cook until *al dente*, according to the timings on the package.

Drain the pasta and return it to the warm pan. Add the roasted pumpkin or squash. Slice or chop the mozzarella butter and add to the pasta. Toss, divide between 4 bowls or plates, top with sage leaves, and serve.

simple spaghetti with capers and olives

Don't be tempted to add oil to the pasta-cooking water—it is a myth that it keeps pasta from sticking and is a waste of good oil! Just make sure you stir occasionally with a wooden fork or spoon while it is cooking.

12 oz. dried spaghetti

⅓ cup virgin olive oil

2 garlic cloves, finely chopped

2 tablespoons capers, drained and rinsed, plus a few caperberries (optional)

12 kalamata olives, pitted and chopped

freshly squeezed juice of ½ unwaxed lemon

½ cup chopped flat-leaf parsley

sea salt and freshly ground black pepper

shavings of fresh Parmesan cheese, to serve (optional)

SERVES 4

Bring a large saucepan of water to a boil. Add a good pinch of salt, then the pasta, and cook until *al dente*, according to the timings on the package.

While the spaghetti is cooking, gently heat the oil in a small saucepan. Add the garlic and cook for 1 minute. Add the capers, caperberries if using, olives, and lemon juice and cook for a further 30 seconds. When the pasta is cooked, drain and return it to the warm pan. Add the caper mixture and parsley and toss well to coat. Add freshly ground black pepper and Parmesan shavings, if using, and serve.

1 block of silken tofu,
about 12 oz.

1 sachet instant dashi
broth powder

2 scallions, cut into thirds

5 tablespoons light soy sauce

3 tablespoons mirin
(sweetened Japanese rice
wine) or dry sherry

1 tablespoon dark sesame oil

2–3 tablespoons peanut or
safflower oil

16 shiitake mushrooms,
stalks trimmed

2 tablespoons cornstarch,
seasoned with salt

8 oz. soba noodles, cooked
for 2 minutes if fresh
and 4 minutes if dried,
until *al dente*

TO SERVE

baby pink or yellow
oyster mushrooms

1 tablespoon sesame seeds,
toasted in a dry skillet

SERVES 4

Texture. Flavor. Color. This Japanese dish has it all. Baby oyster mushrooms are best uncooked to keep their fragile texture, mosslike aroma, and subtle color intact. To toast sesame seeds, put them in a dry skillet and heat gently, tossing regularly to keep them from scorching.

pink oyster and shiitake mushrooms
with crisp tofu and soba noodles

Cut the tofu into 12 rectangular blocks. Line a plate with 3 paper towels and put the tofu on top to drain for at least 30 minutes.

Put 1 quart water in a saucepan and bring to a boil. Stir in the dashi powder, then add the scallions, 3 tablespoons of the soy sauce, and 1 tablespoon of the mirin or dry sherry. Cover with a lid and simmer while you prepare the remaining ingredients.

Put the sesame oil in a skillet, add 1 tablespoon peanut oil, and heat gently. Add the shiitake mushrooms and sauté until lightly browned all over. Add the remaining 2 tablespoons soy sauce, 2 tablespoons mirin, and 3 tablespoons of the prepared dashi broth, bring to a boil, and reduce until syrupy.

Put 1–2 tablespoons peanut oil in a skillet and heat well. Dust the drained blocks of tofu with the seasoned cornstarch, add to the pan, and sauté on all sides until crisp.

Divide the cooked noodles between 4 warm bowls, pour over the hot broth (this will reheat the noodles), top with the cooked mushrooms, crisp tofu, fresh oyster mushrooms, and toasted sesame seeds, then serve.

vegetable noodle stir-fry

4 oz. thin noodles, such as egg noodles

¼ cup peanut or safflower oil

1 garlic clove, crushed

2 inches fresh ginger, finely chopped

1 onion, thinly sliced

1 chile, finely chopped

2 bok choy, about 8 oz., coarsely chopped

1 leek, cut into strips

4 oz. bean sprouts, about 2 cups

1½ cups sliced mushrooms, about 8 oz.

3 tablespoons soy sauce

freshly squeezed juice of 1 unwaxed lime

a bunch of cilantro, chopped

SERVES 4

When making this dish, prepare all the vegetables in advance, so the stir-fry can be quickly and easily put together. Don't overcook the vegetables—they are better when crunchy and brightly colored. You can change the vegetables according to what you have available, but always use the onion, garlic, ginger, and chile.

Bring a large saucepan of water to a boil. Add the noodles and cook for 1 minute if fresh or 3 minutes if dried. Drain them thoroughly.

Heat the sunflower or peanut oil in a wok. Add the garlic, ginger, onion, and chile and cook over medium heat, stirring constantly, until softened.

Add the bok choy, leek, bean sprouts, and mushrooms to the wok and stir-fry for 2–3 minutes.

Add the soy sauce, lime juice, and noodles and use 2 spoons to mix the vegetables and noodles together. Divide between 4 bowls, top with the chopped cilantro, and serve immediately.

poached mushrooms with egg noodles

4 cremini mushrooms

4 scallions, trimmed

4 shallots

2 fresh bay leaves

8 oz. dried egg noodles

2 zucchini, sliced crosswise

4 oz. baby corn, trimmed

4 oz. green beans or Chinese long beans, sliced, about 1 cup

4 oz. spinach, chopped, about 1 cup

1 tablespoon soy sauce

sea salt and freshly ground black pepper

SERVES 4

The purity and natural flavors of this noodle dish will make you feel very healthy! You can use tofu instead of mushrooms, if you prefer.

Put the mushrooms in a large saucepan and add the scallions, shallots, bay leaves, salt, and pepper. Add water to cover and heat until simmering. Cover with a lid and cook for 20 minutes.

Add the noodles to the pan of vegetables, and extra water to cover if necessary. Add the zucchini, corn, beans, spinach, and soy sauce. Simmer for a further 4 minutes, until the noodles and vegetables are cooked. Remove the bay leaves and discard.

Serve the vegetables and noodles in 4 bowls with a ladle of the cooking juices poured over.

This is the perfect healthy choice when you have a number of mouths to feed—it serves 6 people and takes only a matter of minutes to prepare and cook. Other vegetables can always be added, such as asparagus, thin green beans, carrots, baby corn, mushrooms, or water chestnuts, whatever you have on hand.

noodle mountain

6 oz. thin dried egg noodles

¼ cup peanut or safflower oil

2 garlic cloves, chopped

2 inches fresh ginger, peeled and chopped

2 onions, thinly sliced

2 chiles, finely chopped

½ Napa cabbage, finely shredded

4 oz. bean sprouts, about 2 cups

¼ cup soy sauce

freshly squeezed juice of 2 limes

1 bunch of scallions, chopped

8 oz. cashews, chopped, about 2 cups

SERVES 6

Cook the noodles in a large saucepan of boiling water for 3–5 minutes, drain, and transfer to a bowl of cold water. Set aside.

Heat the oil in a wok and add the garlic, ginger, onions, and chiles. Cook over medium heat for 5 minutes until softened. Add the cabbage and bean sprouts and stir briefly.

Drain the noodles well and add to the wok. Toss with 2 large spoons, then add the soy sauce, lime juice, scallions, and cashews. Mix well and serve immediately.

vegetable couscous

2 tablespoons olive oil
2 onions, cut into wedges
2 shallots, peeled
3 garlic cloves, chopped
1 fresh red chile, chopped
1 teaspoon paprika
½ teaspoon ground cinnamon
½ teaspoon coriander seeds, crushed
½ teaspoon cumin seeds, crushed
4 cardamom pods, crushed
a large pinch of saffron threads
3 carrots, cut into 1-inch chunks
2 parsnips, cut into 1-inch chunks
½ butternut squash, cut into 1-inch chunks
2 zucchini, thickly sliced
15 oz. canned plum tomatoes, about 2 cups
2½ cups Vegetable Broth (page 233)
15 oz. canned chickpeas, about 2 cups, rinsed and drained
⅔ cup golden raisins, 4 oz.
sea salt and freshly ground black pepper
a bunch of cilantro, chopped, to serve

PINE NUT COUSCOUS
2½ cups couscous, 1 lb.
¾ cup pine nuts
4 tablespoons unsalted butter, melted

SERVES 4

I think this is especially good for a large gathering of people, young and old. Don't be put off by the long list of ingredients—once in the pot, it looks after itself.

Heat the olive oil in a large saucepan. Add the onions, shallots, garlic, and chile and cook for 2 minutes. Add the paprika, cinnamon, coriander seeds, cumin seeds, cardamom, and saffron and cook for a further 3 minutes.

Add the carrots, parsnips, butternut squash, and zucchini. Cook for 5 minutes, stirring well to coat the vegetables with the spices.

Add the canned tomatoes, broth, chickpeas, golden raisins, salt, and pepper. Make sure all the vegetables are covered with liquid—add extra broth or water as necessary. Bring to a boil and simmer for 20 minutes.

Pour the couscous in a saucepan and add enough boiling water to cover it by 1 inch. Bring to a boil and simmer the couscous for 3 minutes, stirring frequently. Drain well.

Put the pine nuts in a dry skillet and cook over medium heat, stirring constantly, until browned. Add to the drained couscous.

Pour the melted butter over the couscous and season with salt and pepper. Fluff up the grains with a fork and transfer to a large serving bowl.

Top the couscous with the cooked vegetable mixture and sprinkle with a generous quantity of chopped fresh cilantro. Serve hot.

rice

Wonderful produce from a local market in Umbria inspired this risotto. Small, garden-fresh zucchini and milky white, fluffy ricotta cheese are essential. Italian stores and some supermarkets sell fresh ricotta.

risotto with zucchini and ricotta

1 stick unsalted butter

4 small zucchini, chopped

a handful of fresh mint leaves, torn

a handful of fresh flat-leaf parsley, chopped

1 quart Vegetable Broth (page 233)

1 tablespoon olive oil

8 shallots, finely chopped

2 garlic cloves, crushed

1½ cups risotto rice, such as vialone nano, carnaroli, or arborio

½ cup white wine

⅓ cup fresh ricotta cheese or cottage cheese, drained, 3 oz.

2 cups freshly grated Parmesan cheese

sea salt and freshly ground black pepper

SERVES 4

Melt half the butter in a skillet, add the zucchini, and cook over medium heat until tender, about 5 minutes. Add the mint and parsley and mix well. Set aside.

Put the broth in a saucepan. Heat until almost boiling, then reduce the heat until barely simmering to keep it hot.

Heat the remaining butter and the oil in a deep skillet or heavy saucepan over medium heat. Add the shallots and cook for 1–2 minutes, until softened but not browned. Add the garlic and mix well.

Add the rice and stir with a wooden spoon until the grains are well coated and glistening, about 1 minute. Pour in the wine and stir continuously until it has been completely absorbed.

Add 1 ladle of hot broth and simmer, stirring until the liquid has been absorbed. Continue to add the broth at intervals and cook as before, until all the liquid has been absorbed and the rice is tender but still firm, about 18–20 minutes.

Add the cooked zucchini, ricotta, Parmesan, salt, and pepper. Mix well. Remove from the heat, cover, and let rest for 2 minutes.

Spoon into warm bowls and serve immediately.

rice balls

3½ cups Vegetable Broth (page 233)

4 tablespoons unsalted butter

1½ cups risotto rice, such as vialone nano, carnaroli, or arborio

6 oz. fresh mozzarella cheese, drained and cut into small cubes

6 shallots, finely chopped

a handful of mixed fresh herbs, such as parsley, basil, and oregano, chopped

finely grated zest of 1 large unwaxed orange

½ cup freshly grated Parmesan cheese

⅓ cup olive oil

sea salt and freshly ground black pepper

BREAD CRUMB COATING

1 egg, lightly beaten

1 cup fresh bread crumbs

MAKES 8

These cheesy rice balls, known as *supplì al telefono*, are enjoyed throughout Italy. In Sicily they are called *arancini*, meaning "little oranges". This is a good way of using risotto to make delicious party food or antipasto.

Put the broth in a saucepan. Heat until almost boiling, then reduce the heat until barely simmering to keep it hot.

Melt the butter in a wide saucepan. Add the rice and stir, using a wooden spoon, until the grains are well coated and glistening, about 1 minute. Add 1 ladle of hot broth and simmer, stirring until it has been absorbed. Continue to add the broth at intervals and cook as before, until all the liquid has been absorbed and the rice is tender but still firm, about 18–20 minutes.

Add the mozzarella, shallots, mixed herbs, orange zest, Parmesan, salt, and pepper. Mix well. Remove from the heat and let cool. The rice is easier to handle and shape when it is cold.

Using your hands, shape the flavored rice into 8 balls. Dip each one in the beaten egg and coat well, then roll them in the bread crumbs, pressing crumbs onto any uncovered areas.

Heat the oil in a skillet, add the rice balls (in batches, if necessary), and cook until golden on all sides, about 8 minutes. Drain well on paper towels. Serve hot or cold.

They say that a risotto should be constantly stirred, but this isn't absolutely necessary. Time is too short. Stir it frequently, but you can get on with something else in the kitchen at the same time.

mushroom risotto

1 quart Vegetable Broth
(page 233)

2 oz. dried mushrooms such as
chanterelle, morel, shiitake,
or porcini

1 tablespoon olive oil

4 tablespoons unsalted butter

1 garlic clove, chopped

1 onion, finely chopped

1½ cups risotto rice, such as
vialone nano, carnaroli,
or arborio

⅓ cup dry white wine

1 cup freshly grated Parmesan
cheese, plus 3 oz. extra,
shaved or grated, to serve

sea salt and freshly ground
black pepper

SERVES 4

Put the broth and dried mushrooms in a saucepan and let soak for 10 minutes. Then slowly heat the broth to simmering point. Strain the mushrooms and return the broth to the saucepan to keep hot.

Melt the oil and half the butter in a large saucepan. Add the garlic and onion and cook over medium heat until softened but not browned. Add the rice and stir until all the grains are coated with butter and oil.

Add 1 ladle of hot broth to the rice and mix well. When the rice has absorbed the liquid, add another ladle of broth and stir well. Repeat with the remaining broth, cooking the risotto for 15–20 minutes until all the liquid has been absorbed. Meanwhile, chop the mushrooms into smaller pieces as necessary.

Add the soaked mushrooms, white wine, the remaining butter, and the grated Parmesan to the risotto. Season to taste with salt and pepper and mix gently over the heat for 2 minutes. Serve with a separate dish of shaved or grated cheese to sprinkle over the top.

crusted golden rice bake

This style of rice is inspired by the method used in Iran—crunchy rice is delicious and makes a sensational change from the white and fluffy rice that we know here.

1 cup basmati rice

3 tablespoons olive oil

2 onions, chopped

2 garlic cloves, chopped

1 cup dried apricots, chopped, about 6 oz.

½ cup slivered almonds, toasted in a dry skillet

1 teaspoon ground turmeric

1 teaspoon cardamom pods, crushed

1 tablespoon garam masala*

1 stick unsalted butter, cut into small pieces

sea salt and freshly ground black pepper

an ovenproof skillet, buttered

SERVES 4

Put the rice in a large bowl, wash it in several changes of cold water, drain, then cover with cold water and let soak for 3 hours.

When ready to cook, bring a large saucepan of water to a boil. Add the rice, stir well, return to a simmer, and cook for 5 minutes.

Drain the rice and fill the pan with cold water to stop it from cooking any more. When cold, drain well.

Heat the olive oil in a saucepan, add the onions and garlic, and cook for 5 minutes without letting them brown. Add the apricots, toasted almonds, turmeric, cardamom, garam masala, salt, and pepper, and mix well.

Stir the spiced onions into the rice, then transfer it to the prepared skillet and smooth over the top. Dot with butter and cover tightly with foil.

Cook in a preheated oven at 350°F for 45 minutes, then remove the foil and cook for a further 15 minutes.

Remove from the oven, cover with a large plate, and quickly invert both skillet and plate. Remove the skillet to reveal the rice with its golden crust.

*Note: Garam masala is a spice blend that originates from northern India—*Garam* means "hot" and *masala* means "spice". It is available from Asian stores and larger supermarkets.

A great favorite in Northern Italy where pumpkin is eaten all year round, not just in the fall. Pumpkins vary enormously—the best ones to use are the smaller pie pumpkins otherwise use butternut squash.

pumpkin risotto

1 quart Vegetable Broth (page 233)

4 tablespoons unsalted butter

1 tablespoon olive oil

8 shallots, finely chopped

2 garlic cloves, crushed

1½ cups risotto rice, such as vialone nano, carnaroli, or arborio

½ cup white wine

2 cups chopped pumpkin or butternut squash, about 8 oz.

a handful of fresh flat-leaf parsley, chopped

5 oz. freshly grated Parmesan cheese, 1½ cups

sea salt and freshly ground black pepper

SERVES 4

Put the broth in a saucepan. Heat until almost boiling, then reduce the heat until barely simmering to keep it hot.

Heat the butter and oil in a deep skillet or heavy-bottomed saucepan over medium heat. Add the shallots and cook for 1–2 minutes, until softened but not browned. Add the garlic and mix well.

Add the rice and stir with a wooden spoon until the grains are well coated and glistening, about 1 minute. Pour in the wine and stir until it has been completely absorbed.

Add 1 ladle of hot broth, the pumpkin or butternut squash, and parsley. Simmer, stirring until the liquid has been absorbed. Continue to add the broth at intervals and cook as before, until the liquid has been absorbed, the pumpkin is cooked, and the rice is tender but firm, about 18–20 minutes. Reserve the last ladle of broth.

Add the reserved broth, Parmesan, salt, and pepper. Mix well. Remove from the heat, cover, and let rest for 2 minutes.

Spoon into warm bowls and serve immediately.

I like the simplicity of this dish—this is probably why it's popular with children as well as grown-ups. It's almost impossible to imagine Italian food without tomatoes—use firm, red, sun-ripened tomatoes with a fruity scent.

tomato risotto

1 quart Vegetable Broth (page 233)

4 tablespoons unsalted butter

1 tablespoon olive oil

8 shallots, finely chopped

2 garlic cloves, crushed

1½ cups risotto rice, such as vialone nano, carnaroli, or arborio

⅓ cup white wine

8 firm tomatoes, seeded and coarsely chopped

5 oz. freshly grated Parmesan cheese, 1½ cups, plus extra to serve

a large handful of fresh basil leaves, torn

sea salt and freshly ground black pepper

SERVES 4

Put the broth in a saucepan. Heat until almost boiling, then reduce the heat until barely simmering to keep it hot.

Heat the butter and olive oil in a deep skillet or heavy saucepan over medium heat. Add the shallots and cook for 1–2 minutes, until softened but not browned. Add the garlic and mix well.

Add the rice and stir with a wooden spoon until the grains are well coated and glistening, about 1 minute. Pour in the wine and stir until it has been completely absorbed.

Add 1 ladle of hot broth and simmer, stirring until it has been absorbed. Repeat. After 10 minutes, add the tomatoes. Continue to add the broth at intervals and cook as before, for a further 8–10 minutes, until the liquid has been absorbed and the tomatoes and rice are tender but still firm. Reserve the last ladle of broth.

Add the reserved broth, Parmesan, basil, salt, and pepper. Mix well. Remove from the heat, cover, and let rest for 2 minutes.

Spoon into warm bowls, sprinkle with some freshly grated Parmesan, and serve immediately.

artichoke risotto

4 small or 2 large globe artichokes

1 lemon, halved

1 quart Vegetable Broth (page 233)

4 tablespoons unsalted butter

1 tablespoon olive oil

8 shallots, finely chopped

1 garlic clove, crushed

1½ cups risotto rice, such as vialone nano, carnaroli, or arborio

⅓ cup white wine

5 oz. freshly grated Parmesan cheese, 1½ cups, plus extra to serve

2 tablespoons mascarpone cheese

a handful of fresh flat-leaf parsley, coarsely chopped

sea salt and freshly ground black pepper

SERVES 4

Try to buy young artichokes with long, uncut stems. The shorter the stem, the tougher the artichoke tends to be. Young artichokes are also less fibrous. Firmly closed artichokes are an indication of freshness; if the leaves are open they are old.

To prepare the artichokes, pull off the tough outer leaves and cut off the spiky, pointed top. Remove the stalk and cut each artichoke lengthwise into 4 segments if small or 8 segments if large. Cut away the fuzzy, prickly choke. Squeeze the lemon over the segments to prevent discoloration. Set aside.

Put the broth in a saucepan. Heat until almost boiling, then reduce the heat until barely simmering to keep it hot.

Heat the butter and oil in a deep skillet or heavy saucepan over medium heat. Add the shallots and cook for 1–2 minutes, until softened but not browned. Add the garlic and artichoke segments and cook for 2–3 minutes.

Add the rice and stir with a wooden spoon until the grains are well coated and glistening, about 1 minute. Pour in the wine and stir continuously until it has been completely absorbed.

Add 1 ladle of hot broth and simmer, stirring until it has been absorbed. Continue to add the broth at intervals and cook as before, until the liquid has been absorbed and the rice is tender but firm, about 18–20 minutes.

Add the Parmesan, mascarpone, parsley, salt, and pepper. Mix well. Remove from the heat, cover, and let rest for 2 minutes.

Spoon into warm bowls and serve with grated Parmesan.

beans, lentils, and chickpeas

white bean and tomato salad

1½ lb. new potatoes, unpeeled

1½ lb. canned white beans, about 4 cups, drained and rinsed

4 ripe tomatoes, quartered

4 scallions, sliced

a bunch of flat-leaf parsley, chopped

¼ cup extra virgin olive oil

freshly squeezed juice of 1 lemon

sea salt and freshly ground black pepper

SERVES 8

This is a lovely fresh summer salad and perfect for eating *al fresco*. You could serve it as an accompaniment for grills or on its own with some fresh country bread as a light lunch.

Cook the potatoes in a large saucepan of lightly salted boiling water for about 20 minutes, or until tender when pierced with a knife. Drain. When cool enough to handle, cut into wedges and put in a large bowl.

Add the beans, tomatoes, scallions, and parsley. Sprinkle with olive oil, lemon juice, salt, and pepper. Toss gently and serve.

avocado and chickpea salad

2 eggs

8 oz. baby spinach,
about 2 cups

15 oz. canned chickpeas,
about 2 cups, drained
and rinsed

2 ripe avocados, halved,
pitted, sliced, and peeled

2 teaspoons sweet Spanish
paprika

bread such as ciabatta or
focaccia, to serve

CREAMY CHIVE DRESSING

freshly squeezed juice of
1 lemon

3 tablespoons milk

2 tablespoons plain yogurt

a bunch of chives, chopped

sea salt and freshly ground
black pepper

SERVES 4

This is a fresh, instant meal for lazy evenings. When buying avocados, make sure they are slightly soft to the touch and blemish-free.

Put the eggs in a small saucepan of water, bring to a boil, and simmer for 8–9 minutes, until hard-cooked. Drain, cool in cold water, peel, then cut into quarters and set aside.

To make the dressing, put the lemon juice in a bowl with the milk, yogurt, and chopped chives. Season generously with salt and pepper and stir until smooth.

Put the spinach, chickpeas, avocados, and eggs in a bowl. Sprinkle with the sweet paprika, then spoon the dressing over the top. Serve with fresh bread.

white and green bean salad

The ingredients for this salad are very flexible: cannellini beans or chickpeas could be used in place of the lima beans, and other green beans or peas—such as snowpeas, sugar snaps, or sliced runner beans—in place of the regular green beans.

3 tablespoons olive oil

1 tablespoon balsamic vinegar

1½ lb. canned lima beans, about 4 cups, drained and rinsed

8 oz. green beans, trimmed

½ cup pumpkin seeds

sea salt and freshly ground black pepper

SERVES 8

Put the oil and vinegar in a large serving bowl. Stir in the lima beans and set aside.

Cook the green beans in a saucepan of lightly salted boiling water for 3 minutes. Drain, refresh in several changes of cold water until cool, then drain again.

Add the green beans and pumpkin seeds to the bowl and stir. Sprinkle with salt and pepper and serve.

I have a passion for chickpeas, but have found that most people don't really know what to do with them. Using the canned variety, as in this super Mediterranean-style salad, dispenses with the soaking that is needed with dried beans.

chickpea, tomato, and pepper salad

5 plum tomatoes, halved and seeded

3 large red bell peppers, halved and seeded

15 oz. canned chickpeas, about 2 cups, drained and rinsed

a bunch of flat-leaf parsley, chopped

sea salt and freshly ground black pepper

extra virgin olive oil, to serve

SERVES 4

Put the tomatoes and bell peppers in a lightly oiled roasting pan. Cook in a preheated oven at 375°F for 20 minutes.

Remove the pan from the oven and transfer the tomatoes and peppers to a bowl. Add the drained chickpeas, then mix in the parsley and seasoning.

Transfer the salad to a serving dish, sprinkle with a little olive oil, then serve at room temperature.

warm mediterranean lentil salad

10 cherry tomatoes,
about 1 cup

1½ cups brown lentils, 10 oz.

grated zest and juice of
1 unwaxed lemon

1 fresh bay leaf

2 garlic cloves, crushed
and chopped

2 red onions, chopped

½ cup pitted olives, such as
Kalamata

a bunch of flat-leaf parsley,
chopped

¼ cup extra virgin olive oil

sea salt and freshly ground
black pepper

4 oz. fresh Parmesan cheese,
cut into shavings, or mozzarella
cheese, sliced, to serve

a baking tray, lightly oiled

SERVES 4

Really, this is a salad for all seasons. It works
wonderfully served warm or cold and is bound
to become a regular feature on your table.

Preheat the oven to 250°F. Put the cherry tomatoes on the
prepared baking tray and cook in the oven for 40 minutes.

Put the lentils in a saucepan. Add the lemon zest and juice,
bay leaf, garlic, and enough water to cover. Stir, bring to
a boil, then simmer for 40 minutes or until the lentils are soft.

Drain the lentils thoroughly and transfer to a large bowl. Add
the cherry tomatoes, red onions, olives, parsley, olive oil, salt,
and pepper. Toss gently, then serve topped with slices of
Parmesan or mozzarella.

curried lentils and spinach

¼ cup olive oil

1 onion, chopped

1 garlic clove, chopped

1 teaspoon ground cumin or garam masala

1 teaspoon medium-hot curry powder

½ teaspoon cardamom pods, crushed

1½ cups brown lentils, 10 oz.

2 tomatoes, peeled and chopped

8 oz. spinach, cut into ribbons, about 2 cups

freshly squeezed juice of 1 lemon

sea salt and freshly ground black pepper

SERVES 4

This dish is really delicious, all the flavors bring the lentils to life. If you need some comfort food then try this, it's so easy, too.

Heat the oil in a medium saucepan, add the onion, and cook for 5 minutes. Add the garlic, cumin or garam masala, curry powder, and cardamom, mix well, then cook for 3 minutes.

Add the brown lentils and 2 cups water to the pan, bring to a boil, reduce the heat, and simmer for about 20 minutes, stirring frequently.

When the lentils are soft, add the tomatoes, spinach, lemon juice, salt, and pepper. Stir well and serve hot or just warm.

one-dish meals

roasted pumpkin, red onions, baby potatoes, and fennel
with chickpeas in tomato sauce

1 butternut squash or ½ pumpkin, cut into wedges, skin left on and seeds left in

3 red onions, cut into wedges

8 baby new potatoes, halved

2 fennel bulbs, trimmed and cut into wedges

3 tablespoons olive oil

15 oz. canned chickpeas, about 2 cups, drained and rinsed

sea salt and freshly ground black pepper

PARMESAN COOKIES

10 oz. Parmesan cheese, grated, about 3½ cups

TOMATO SAUCE

2 tablespoons olive oil

1 onion, chopped

2 celery stalks, chopped

1 leek, trimmed and chopped

1 garlic clove, chopped

15 oz. canned chopped tomatoes, about 2 cups

1 tablespoon tomato paste

½ cup red wine

sea salt and freshly ground black pepper

a baking tray, lined with baking parchment

SERVES 4

An easy dish. The tomato sauce can be made the day before it's needed—in fact, it actually improves overnight.

To make the Parmesan cookies, pile teaspoons of the grated Parmesan on the lined baking tray and flatten gently to make equal rounds. Bake in a preheated oven at 375°F for 5 minutes. Remove the paper from the baking tray with the cookies still on it. Replace with another sheet of paper and repeat with the remaining cheese. Let cool.

Put the squash, onion, potato, and fennel in a roasting pan. Add the oil and sprinkle with salt and pepper. Toss to coat, then roast in a preheated oven at 400°F for 45 minutes, checking after 30 minutes that the vegetables are cooking evenly and turning them if needed. Add the chickpeas and roast for a further 5–10 minutes until all the vegetables are browned and tender.

To make the tomato sauce, heat the oil in a saucepan. Add the onion, celery, leek, and garlic and sauté for 5 minutes until soft. Add the tomatoes, tomato paste, and red wine. Simmer gently for 30 minutes, adding a little more red wine if the sauce becomes too thick. Using a stick blender, process until smooth. Add salt and pepper to taste, pour over the roasted vegetables, and serve with the Parmesan cookies.

4 parsnips

1 butternut squash, peeled
and seeded

¼ cup olive oil

1 small onion, finely chopped

1 garlic clove, finely chopped

1¾ cups unsweetened
canned coconut milk

⅔ cup heavy cream

a pinch of sugar

⅓ cup walnut halves,
about 1½ oz.

sea salt and freshly ground
mixed peppercorns

fresh cilantro leaves, to serve

CURRY SPICE MIX

1½ tablespoons cumin seeds

1 tablespoon coriander seeds

1–2 teaspoons caraway seeds

black seeds from 4 green
cardamom pods, crushed

2 star anise

½ tablespoon fenugreek seeds

½ teaspoon freshly
grated nutmeg

1 tablespoon mild
curry powder

1 garlic clove, crushed

olive oil, for binding

SERVES 4

You won't need all of the curry spice mix for this dish,
so put any extra in a screwtop jar and refrigerate. It is
wonderful added to sauces or marinades.

curried parsnips and squash
with walnuts

To make the curry mix, grind the spice seeds and star anise to a powder
in a spice mill or coffee grinder. Put in a small bowl and add the nutmeg,
curry powder and garlic. Mix in enough oil to make a paste.

Cut the parsnips and squash into equal pieces. Heat half the oil in
skillet, add the vegetables, and toss quickly to coat. Season lightly,
then transfer to an ovenproof dish.

In the same skillet, heat the remaining oil and sauté the onion and garlic
until soft. Add 1 tablespoon of the curry paste and cook to release the
aromas. Add the coconut milk and cream. Season with salt and pepper
to taste and add the sugar. Heat gently, then pour the sauce over the
vegetables. Cover with foil and cook in a preheated oven at 350°F for
about 45 minutes or until the vegetables are tender.

Remove from the oven and sprinkle the vegetables with the walnuts.
Return to the oven and cook, uncovered, for about 15–20 minutes, until
the vegetables are golden and the sauce has caramelized slightly. Serve
sprinkled with cilantro.

Fresh oregano is used throughout the Mediterranean and gives this dish a warm, earthy flavor. If you can't get it, use flat-leaf parsley or chives instead. Flowering herbs look so beautiful and taste fabulous too, so when in season, serve the vegetables with a sprinkling of purple oregano petals.

vegetable tian
with mozzarella and oregano

2 yellow bell peppers

⅓ cup olive oil

1 long, thin eggplant, cut into thick slices

2 red onions, cut into quarters

2 medium zucchini, cut diagonally into chunks

12 garlic cloves

1 cup red wine

12 ripe plum tomatoes, cut in half lengthwise

12 black olives, pitted

2 tablespoons balsamic vinegar

1 tablespoon chopped fresh oregano

10 oz. mozzarella cheese, drained and thickly sliced

sea salt and freshly ground black pepper

crusty country bread, to serve

SERVES 4

Roast the bell peppers under a hot broiler or in the preheated oven for 15–20 minutes or until the skins are charred and blackened. Put them in a plastic bag, seal, and let cool. Peel the peppers (the skin will come off easily), then cut them in half, and scrape out and discard the seeds. Cut the flesh into thick strips. Set aside.

Heat the oil in a skillet, add the eggplant, and sauté briefly. Remove to a plate. In the same skillet, sauté the onions, zucchini, and garlic until just golden. Remove to a plate.

Add the wine to the skillet and heat gently, stirring to deglaze the pan juices.

Put the prepared vegetables and plum tomatoes in a shallow, ovenproof dish. Sprinkle with the olives and pour in the heated wine. Sprinkle with the balsamic vinegar and half the oregano. Season with salt and pepper.

Bake in a preheated oven at 400°F for 20 minutes. Remove from the oven, dot the top with the mozzarella, and cook for a further 10–15 minutes or until the cheese has melted and the vegetables are well roasted.

Top with the remaining oregano and serve with crusty country bread to mop up the lovely juices.

chickpea and vegetable curry

3 tablespoons peanut or safflower oil

2 garlic cloves, crushed

2 red onions, chopped

2 inches fresh ginger, peeled and finely chopped

1 tablespoon curry powder

2 teaspoons ground coriander

½ teaspoon fenugreek (optional)

½ teaspoon hot red pepper flakes

15 oz. canned chopped tomatoes, about 2 cups

1½ lb. potatoes, cut into 1-inch pieces

1 cauliflower, cut into florets

1½ lb. canned chickpeas, about 4 cups, drained and rinsed

1 lb. spinach, about 4 cups, chopped

8 oz. okra, washed, dried, and halved lengthwise, about 2 cups

TO SERVE

naan bread

pappadams

SERVES 12

This curry is very simple to make and you can change any of the vegetables to suit availability. As with all curries, this can be made in advance and left overnight for the flavors to deepen and intensify. You could serve it with the Crusted Golden Rice Bake on page 167.

Heat the oil in a large saucepan, add the garlic, onion, and ginger, and cook over low heat for 10 minutes until softened. Add the curry powder, coriander, fenugreek, if using, and pepper flakes, mix well, and cook for another 4 minutes.

Add the tomatoes and ½ cup water, then add the potatoes, cauliflower, and chickpeas. Mix well, cover with a lid, and simmer for 15 minutes, stirring frequently.

Add the spinach and okra, mix well, and simmer for about 5 minutes. You may need to add a little extra water at this final stage. Serve with naan bread and pappadams.

potato, sage, and apple gratin

3 lb. salad potatoes, thinly sliced

1 onion, finely chopped

leaves from 3–4 sprigs of sage

1 tablespoon unsalted butter

4 Granny Smith apples, peeled and thickly sliced

1 cup heavy cream

1 egg

a large pinch of freshly grated nutmeg

sea salt and freshly ground black pepper

6-cup gratin dish, greased

SERVES 4 AS A MAIN DISH

Cook the potatoes in a saucepan of lightly salted boiling water for 5 minutes. Drain and let cool for a few minutes.

Put a layer of potatoes in the gratin dish and top with a layer of chopped onions. Add a few sage leaves, salt, and pepper. Repeat, finishing with a layer of potatoes.

Melt the butter in a skillet, add the apples, and turn to coat well. Arrange the apples on top of the potatoes, slightly overlapping each slice. Put the cream and egg in a bowl and beat well. Beat in the nutmeg, salt, and pepper. Pour over the apples.

Bake in a preheated oven at 375°F for about 1 hour, or until the potatoes are tender—test by piercing the center with a skewer. Remove from the oven.

For a golden, nutty top, put the gratin under a hot broiler for a couple of minutes.

Perfect for the busy cook, the vegetables can be layered ahead of time, then topped with the apples before baking. The gratin is delicious on its own or served with vegetarian sausages.

Teriyaki is a Japanese glaze made from sake or mirin (rice wines), shoyu (Japanese soy sauce), and sugar. It is available from large supermarkets or Asian food stores.

honey teriyaki vegetables

2 teaspoons peanut or safflower oil

a bunch of radishes, trimmed, and halved lengthwise

4 carrots, sliced diagonally

a bunch of scallions, halved crosswise

1 cup snowpeas, halved lengthwise, about 4 oz.

1 tablespoon sesame seeds, toasted in a dry skillet, to serve

DRESSING

1 tablespoon honey

2 tablespoons teriyaki sauce

freshly ground black pepper

SERVES 4

To make the dressing, put the honey and teriyaki sauce in a small bowl and mix. Add black pepper to taste.

Put the oil in a wok and heat until hot. Add the vegetables and 2 tablespoons water and stir-fry for about 3 minutes, until the vegetables are just heated through but still crisp. Transfer to a warm serving dish.

Reduce the heat, add the dressing to the wok and heat it through gently until just warm. Pour the dressing over the vegetables, sprinkle with the sesame seeds, and serve.

Chickpeas add a nutty flavor and buttery texture. Sautéing the vegetables first will caramelize their natural sugars to give extra flavor. Serve with crusty bread.

1 celery root, about 1 lb.

3 carrots

4 leeks

2 parsnips

12 shallots

4 tablespoons unsalted butter

2 teaspoons brown sugar

15 oz. canned chickpeas, about 2 cups, drained and rinsed

2 cups Vegetable Broth (page 233)

4–5 sprigs of thyme

1 fresh bay leaf, torn in half

sea salt and freshly ground black pepper

TO SERVE

snipped chives

crusty bread (optional)

SERVES 4

braised root vegetables
with chickpeas and thyme

Peel and trim the vegetables, cut into bite-size chunks, but leave the shallots whole.

Heat the butter in a large skillet, add the vegetables, and cook, stirring over high heat until lightly browned. Season with salt and pepper.

Sprinkle with the sugar and cook until the vegetables are slightly caramelized. Transfer to a casserole dish with a lid and add the chickpeas.

Add the broth, thyme, and bay leaf to the skillet and bring to a boil. Pour into the casserole, cover, and cook in a preheated oven at 300°F for 1 hour. Increase to 400°F and cook, uncovered, for about 15–20 minutes until the vegetables are tender and glazed and the cooking liquid has reduced slightly. Season to taste with salt and pepper.

Serve sprinkled with snipped chives and accompanied by crusty bread, if using.

2 tablespoons olive oil

1 large onion, chopped

2 teaspoons brown sugar

3 garlic cloves, crushed

5 small hot dried chiles, soaked in boiling water to cover

3 tablespoons smoked sweet paprika

1 large parsnip, cut into 1-inch cubes

1 large potato, cubed

8 oz. baby carrots, trimmed and halved lengthwise

1½ lb. canned chopped tomatoes, about 3 cups

1¼ cups red wine

15 oz. canned chickpeas, about 2 cups, drained and rinsed

freshly ground black pepper

LEMON AND CUMIN CRACKED WHEAT

1 cup cracked wheat or bulghur, 6 oz.

2 tablespoons virgin olive oil

1 unwaxed lemon, finely chopped

3 teaspoons ground cumin

2 garlic cloves, crushed

freshly ground black pepper

TO SERVE

2 tablespoons plain yogurt or sour cream

a bunch of mint, chopped

SERVES 4

vegetable goulash
with lemon and cumin cracked wheat

Paprika gives Hungarian goulash its appealing reddish color and fragrance. Here the smoked variety, often used in Spanish cooking, adds a distinctive, deep flavor.

Put the oil in a large saucepan and heat. When hot, add the onion, cover with a lid, and cook over medium heat for 10–15 minutes until softened. Remove the lid and stir in the sugar. Increase the heat and cook for 5 minutes until golden.

Add the garlic, drained chiles, and paprika and cook for about 30 seconds. Add all the vegetables, tomatoes, wine, and 1¼ cups water. Bring to a boil, reduce the heat, and simmer, uncovered, for 35–40 minutes until the vegetables are just tender, adding a little extra water if they dry out. Add the chickpeas and some black pepper and simmer for a further 5–10 minutes.

To make the lemon and cumin cracked wheat, put the cracked wheat or bulgur in a bowl and add boiling water to cover. Leave to swell for 15–20 minutes until soft, then drain through a strainer, pressing out excess water.

Heat the oil in a large saucepan. Add the lemon and sauté for 2 minutes, then add the cumin and garlic and sauté for 30 seconds. Add the cracked wheat or bulghur and stir-fry for 1–2 minutes. Add plenty of black pepper.

Transfer the goulash to serving plates and top with the yogurt or sour cream. Sprinkle with the chopped mint and serve with the lemon and cumin cracked wheat.

desserts

honey and almond panna cotta
with watermelon and rosewater salad

1 envelope unflavored vegetarian gelatin (agar agar), 1 tablespoon

¾ cup heavy cream

1 cup plain yogurt, strained

2 tablespoons sugar

6 tablespoons honey, ⅓ cup

½ cup ground almonds

1 vanilla bean, split lengthwise and seeds scraped out

WATERMELON AND ROSEWATER SALAD

8–12 unsprayed pink rose petals

1 free-range egg white, beaten

1 tablespoon sugar

1 small watermelon, about 3 lb., chilled

2 tablespoons rosewater

4 ramekins, lightly oiled and lined with cheesecloth or plastic wrap

SERVES 4

This is a very pretty yet simple dessert. It is the perfect choice if you are entertaining as you can make it in advance. If you don't have individual ramekins, use one large bowl for the panna cotta.

To make the panna cotta, put 3 tablespoons warm water in a small bowl, sprinkle the gelatin evenly over the top, and leave until dissolved, about 5 minutes.

Put the cream in a mixing bowl. Add the yogurt, sugar, and honey and stir until smooth. Mix in the ground almonds, vanilla seeds, and gelatin.

Pour the cream mixture in the prepared ramekins, then chill for 4 hours or until set.

Meanwhile, prepare the watermelon and rosewater salad. Dip the rose petals in the beaten egg white, then dust lightly with sugar, and set aside to dry for 1 hour.

Top and tail the watermelon, then slice it into thin wedges and pick out the seeds. Arrange the slices on a large platter, sprinkle with the rosewater, cover, and chill.

To serve, invert the panna cotta onto 4 small plates, add the watermelon slices, and decorate with the rose petals.

Although not, strictly speaking, a crumble, this dessert has a beautifully crisp topping. If you're not a fan of ginger, try finely grated orange zest instead. Both flavors work equally well with rhubarb.

rhubarb crumble
with ginger and vanilla

1½ lb. fresh rhubarb, cut into 1-inch pieces

3 pieces of crystallized ginger, cut into matchsticks

½ cup sugar

1 vanilla bean, split lengthwise and seeds scraped out

CRUMBLE TOPPING

1 cup slivered almonds, 4 oz., toasted in a dry skillet

4 tablespoons unsalted butter

¼ cup rolled oats

1 cup fresh brown bread crumbs

¼ cup brown sugar

4 individual ovenproof dishes, or a shallow baking dish

SERVES 4

Put the rhubarb, ginger, sugar, and vanilla seeds in a saucepan and cook over gentle heat until the juices run from the rhubarb and it starts to soften. Pour into the ovenproof dishes or baking dish.

To make the topping, put the almonds in a dry skillet and cook, stirring, over gentle heat until lightly golden. Be careful or they may burn. Remove and reserve.

Add the butter to the skillet and heat gently until melted. Add the oats, bread crumbs, and brown sugar. Increase the heat and cook briskly, stirring continuously, until the bread crumbs and oats start to caramelize, brown, and separate. Remove from the skillet and stir in the toasted almonds.

Sprinkle the mixture over the rhubarb, starting at the edges and working toward the middle. Press down firmly. Transfer to a preheated oven at 400°F and cook for about 10 minutes until the topping is crisp and golden (the forced rhubarb is very tender and will finish cooking in this time).

nectarine tart

The combination of crumbly, sweet crusty tart and slivers of juicy nectarines makes for a sensational blend of delicate summer flavors.

1⅔ cups all-purpose flour, plus extra for dusting

2¼ sticks butter, cut into small pieces

1 cup confectioners' sugar, plus extra for dusting

2–3 egg yolks

10–12 nectarines or peaches, about 3 lb.

vanilla ice cream, yogurt and honey, or crème fraîche, to serve

a 9-inch tart pan with removable base

SERVES 6–8

Put the flour, butter, and confectioners' sugar in a food processor and blend until the mixture resembles fine bread crumbs. Add the egg yolks and blend again until it forms a ball. Wrap the dough in plastic wrap and chill in the refrigerator for at least 30 minutes.

Put the dough on a lightly floured work surface and knead briefly to soften. Roll it out into a large circle at least 2 inches wider than the base of the pan.

Use the rolling pin to help you carefully lift up the dough and drape it over the tart pan. Gently press the dough down into the pan, making sure there are no air pockets. This dough is very fragile, but don't despair. Just line your tart pan as best you can, and then add extra pieces of dough to patch up any cracks or holes. Use a sharp knife to trim off the excess. Chill the tart crust for 15 minutes.

Cut the nectarines or peaches in half, twist to remove the pits, then cut the fruit into slices. Remove the chilled tart crust from the fridge and, working from the outside, arrange the nectarine or peach slices in circles on the crust, until all the fruit has been used.

Bake the tart in a preheated oven at 375°F for 30 minutes, then reduce the heat to 300°F and continue cooking for a further 40 minutes until the fruit is tender and golden and the crust is crisp.

Dust the tart with confectioners' sugar then serve hot or cold with good-quality vanilla ice cream, yogurt sprinkled with honey, or sweetened crème fraîche.

Foolproof and very quick to prepare, tiramisù is a wonderful dessert for a large group of people—it can be made in advance, doesn't need cooking or heating, and tastes so delicious that it is universally welcomed. You can present it in individual glasses or one large serving bowl.

tiramisù

50 amaretti cookies, crushed

¾ cup Kahlúa or other coffee liqueur

⅓ cup brandy

½ cup strong black coffee

2 lb. mascarpone cheese

8 free-range eggs, separated

½ cup sugar

8 oz. bitter chocolate, grated, or ¼ cup unsweetened cocoa powder

20 glasses or a 12-inch square serving dish

SERVES 20

Put a quarter of the crushed amaretti cookies in the glasses or serving dish. Mix the Kahlúa with the brandy and coffee in a small bowl and pour a quarter of this mixture into the glasses or serving dish.

Put the mascarpone, egg yolks, and sugar in a bowl and beat until smooth. Put the egg whites in a separate bowl, beat until stiff, then fold them into the mascarpone mixture.

Put a quarter of the mixture over the cookies, then repeat the layers 3 times, finishing with a layer of mascarpone mixture.

Sprinkle the chocolate or cocoa over the top of the tiramisù and refrigerate overnight. Serve chilled or at room temperature.

warm chocolate and coffee dessert

1 teaspoon instant coffee

1¾ sticks unsalted butter

1 cup minus 2 tablespoons sugar

2 extra large eggs

1½ cups all-purpose flour

milk, as needed

½ cup unsweetened cocoa powder

light cream, to serve

CHOCOLATE SAUCE

4 oz. bittersweet chocolate, broken into pieces

1 stick butter

¼ cup sugar

¾ cup heavy cream

a plum pudding mold, 1 quart, buttered

SERVES 8

This dessert can be made in advance, then just reheated when required. Don't scrimp on the chocolate sauce ingredients: they make a thick, rich, and glossy sauce that will become one of your prized favorites. You can also serve it poured over poached pears, ice cream, or other desserts.

Put the coffee in a cup, add 1 teaspoon boiling water, and stir to dissolve. Put 4 inches of water in a saucepan large enough to hold the plum pudding mold. Put the butter and sugar in a bowl and, using an electric mixer, beat until creamy, light, and very pale. Beat in the eggs and coffee.

Sift in the flour and cocoa powder and fold into the butter mixture using a large metal spoon, adding a little milk if the mixture seems very stiff. Transfer to the prepared pudding mold and cover tightly with buttered foil or wax paper. Put in the saucepan of water, cover with a lid, and bring to a boil. Reduce the heat and simmer for 1½ hours, checking the water level from time to time and topping up if necessary.

To make the sauce, put the chocolate, butter, sugar, and cream in a small saucepan. Heat gently, stirring frequently, until melted. Remove from the heat and set aside until ready to serve.

Remove the mold from the saucepan and carefully invert the dessert onto a large plate. Serve hot or warm with the chocolate sauce and light cream.

The sweetness of meringue is offset by the sharpness of the fruit. Feel free to use whatever fruits are in season.

raspberry and passionfruit pavlova

4 extra-large egg whites

a pinch of salt

1¾ cups sugar, plus 2 tablespoons extra

1 tablespoon cornstarch

2 teaspoons freshly squeezed lemon juice

sprigs of mint, to decorate (optional)

FILLING

1⅓ cups heavy cream, whipped

10 oz. raspberries, about 2 cups

3–4 passionfruit

RASPBERRY PURÉE (OPTIONAL)

6 oz. raspberries, about 1½ cups

1–2 tablespoons confectioners' sugar, sifted

a baking tray, lined with parchment paper and sprinkled with cornstarch

SERVES 6–8

Put the egg whites and salt in a large bowl. Using an electric mixer, beat the egg whites until stiff. Gradually add 1¼ cups of the sugar, beating between each addition until the meringue is very glossy and stiff. Beat in the remaining ½ cup sugar.

Sift the reserved sugar and cornstarch together into a small bowl and mix well. Fold half the cornstarch mixture into the meringue, then 1 teaspoon of the lemon juice. Repeat with the remaining cornstarch mixture and lemon juice.

Spoon half the meringue onto the parchment paper and spread out into a circle about 7 inches in diameter. Smooth the top and sides. Spoon the rest of the meringue in a ring around the edge of the circle until the pavlova is about 2½ inches at the edges.

Bake in a preheated oven at 250°F for about 1–1¼ hours. Remove from the oven and let cool. Alternatively, switch off the oven and leave the meringue inside until cool. This will help reduce cracking.

To make the raspberry purée, crush the raspberries with a fork or stick blender, then press through a fine-mesh nylon sieve to make a purée. Discard the seeds. Sweeten to taste with confectioners' sugar.

When the pavlova is cold, carefully remove the parchment paper and put the pavlova on a serving plate. Fill the center with the whipped cream and top with the raspberries. Cut the passionfruit in half and scoop out the pulp and seeds onto the raspberries. Serve decorated with a few sprigs of mint and the raspberry purée, if using.

The quintessential home-style dessert, and the definitive comfort food. It's very simple to make and when served like this—with a caramelized sugar top—it is sophisticated enough for even the most elegant dinner party.

rice pudding
with caramelized pineapple and banana

2 tablespoons unsalted butter

1 tablespoon sugar, plus extra for dusting

½ cup risotto rice, such as vialone nano, carnaroli, or arborio

2 cups milk

1 cup light cream

1 strip of unwaxed lemon zest

a pinch of salt

1 vanilla bean, split in half lengthwise

4 thick slices of fresh pineapple

2 bananas

confectioners' sugar, for dusting

8 wooden skewers, soaked in water for 20 minutes

SERVES 4

Put the butter and sugar in a saucepan and heat until foaming. Stir in the rice, coating the grains until they glisten. In another pan, heat the milk gently until boiling, then gradually add to the rice, stirring. Add the cream, lemon zest, and salt.

Scrape the seeds from the vanilla bean into the rice mixture, then add the bean. Heat until almost boiling, then pour into a deep, ovenproof dish. Cover with parchment paper to prevent a brown skin forming on the top. Bake in a preheated oven at 275°F for 2–2½ hours until creamy and thick.

Remove from the oven and remove the lemon zest and vanilla bean. Spoon the pudding into 4 large ramekins and let cool until lukewarm.

Cut the pineapple and bananas into equal chunks and thread onto the skewers. Sift confectioners' sugar onto the skewered fruit and cook under a hot broiler until the sugar has caramelized. Let cool.

Dust the puddings with a thick layer of confectioners' sugar and sugar and caramelize as before. Let cool until set, then serve the puddings with the caramelized fruit skewers.

crusted lime polenta cake

This is a beautiful moist dessert with a delicious tangy lime kick. Serve it with ice cream rather than mascarpone, if you prefer—coconut ice cream would make a perfect partner for the lime.

2 sticks unsalted butter

1 cup plus 2 tablespoons sugar

3 eggs, beaten

½ teaspoon vanilla extract

2½ cups ground almonds, or 3 cups slivered almonds, ground in a blender

grated zest and juice of 3 unwaxed limes

¾ cup fine yellow cornmeal or polenta flour

1 teaspoon baking powder

a pinch of salt

mascarpone cheese, to serve

LIME CRUST

freshly squeezed juice of 2 limes

3 tablespoons sugar

a springform pan, 10 inches diameter, buttered and floured

SERVES 8–10

Put the butter and sugar in a large bowl and beat with an electric hand mixer until pale and light. Gradually add the eggs, beating all the time. Using a large metal spoon, stir in the vanilla extract and ground almonds, then fold in the lime zest and juice, cornmeal, baking powder, and salt.

Spoon into the prepared cake pan and bake in a preheated oven at 325°F for about 1 hour and 15 minutes or until just set and golden brown.

Meanwhile, to make the lime crust, put the lime juice and sugar in a bowl and mix well.

When the cake is cooked, prick well with a skewer all over the surface and pour over the lime juice mixture. Let cool in the pan for 15 minutes.

Remove the cake from the pan and serve still warm, or let cool completely before slicing. Serve with mascarpone.

basics

Italian pizza makers use a special flour called tipo 00. In America, you can use Italian-style flour made by speciality baking suppliers, such as King Arthur. If you can't find it, unbleached all-purpose flour or bread flour can be used instead. Some cooks add flavorings to the dough, but if you keep it simple the toppings can take center stage.

basic pizza dough

1⅔ cups unbleached all-purpose flour or bread flour, plus extra for sprinkling

½ teaspoon salt

1 package active dry yeast (¼ oz.)

2 tablespoons olive oil

½ cup tepid water

SERVES 4

Put the flour, salt, and yeast in a large bowl and mix. Make a well in the center. Add the oil and water to the well and gradually work in the flour to make a soft dough. Sprinkle with a little flour if the mixture feels too sticky, but make sure it is not too dry: the dough should be pliable and smooth.

Transfer the dough to a lightly floured surface. Knead for 10 minutes, sprinkling with flour when needed, until the dough is smooth and elastic.

Rub some oil over the surface of the dough and return the dough to the bowl. Cover with a clean cloth and leave for about 1 hour, until the dough has doubled in size.

Remove the dough to a lightly floured surface and knead for 2 minutes, until the excess air is punched out. Roll out the dough according to the recipe you are following.

polenta cornmeal dough

To make a cornmeal base, use ⅓ cup fine cornmeal or polenta mixed with 1⅓ cups all-purpose or bread flour.

classic tomato sauce

2 tablespoons olive oil

1 small onion, finely chopped

3 garlic cloves, finely chopped

1½ lb. canned plum tomatoes, about 3½ cups

2 sprigs of fresh rosemary or thyme, or a pinch of dried oregano

a pinch of sugar

sea salt and freshly ground black pepper

MAKES ABOUT 2 CUPS

Heat the oil in a small saucepan, add the onion and garlic, and cook for about 3–4 minutes until softened. Add the tomatoes, breaking them up briefly with a wooden spoon. Add the herbs, sugar, and salt and pepper to taste.

Bring to a boil and partially cover with a lid. Reduce the heat and simmer very gently for 30–60 minutes, stirring from time to time and breaking up the tomatoes with the back of the spoon, until the sauce turns dark red and is reduced by almost half.

Discard any woody herb sprigs. Taste and adjust the seasoning, then let cool slightly before using.

This simple sauce is perfect as a basic topping for almost any pizza or with pasta. Choose canned whole plum tomatoes rather than chopped tomatoes, which can have a bitter edge. Cook the sauce for at least 30 minutes to give it time to develop some richness.

fiery tomato sauce

1½ lb. canned tomato sauce or paste, about 3½ cups

2 tablespoons olive oil

3 garlic cloves, finely chopped

a handful of basil leaves, torn

¼ teaspoon hot red pepper flakes

½ teaspoon sugar

sea salt and freshly ground black pepper

SERVES 4–6

Hot pepper flakes add an extra kick to this smooth, satiny sauce. Use it as an alternative to the Classic Tomato Sauce in any of the pizza recipes in this book. The basil is not essential, but is worth adding if you have some to hand.

Put the tomatoes, oil, garlic, basil, pepper flakes, and sugar in a medium saucepan and add salt and pepper to taste.

Bring to a boil and partially cover with a lid. Reduce the heat and simmer very gently, stirring from time to time, for 30–60 minutes, until the sauce is dark red and reduced by about half.

Taste and adjust the seasoning, if necessary, cover with the lid, and let cool slightly before using.

tomato sauce with double basil

In summer, make this with fresh, ripe tomatoes—otherwise, use canned Italian plum tomatoes. The basil is added in two stages; first for depth of flavor, then at the end for a burst of fresh fragrance. This sauce is delicious served with pasta.

3 tablespoons olive oil

2 garlic cloves, finely chopped

1 shallot, finely chopped

1 cup loosely packed basil leaves

1 lb. ripe tomatoes, chopped, or 15 oz. canned plum tomatoes, about 2 cups

a pinch of sugar

sea salt and freshly ground black pepper

SERVES 4

Heat the oil in a saucepan and add the garlic, shallot, and half the basil. Cook for 3–4 minutes until the shallot is golden.

Add the tomatoes and cook, stirring, for 10 minutes, until thickened and pulpy. Add the sugar, ⅓ cup water, and salt and pepper to taste.

Bring to a boil, cover, and simmer very gently for 1 hour until dark red and thickened, with droplets of oil on the surface.

Tear the remaining basil into the tomato sauce just before serving.

crispy crumbs

These make a great addition to any tomato-based pasta dish.

Heat 1 tablespoon olive oil in a skillet and add 2 cups fresh white bread crumbs. Cook over high heat, stirring until golden brown. The smaller crumbs will go to the bottom of the skillet and char a little, but that's good. Serve straight from the skillet, sprinkled on top of the pasta, while the crumbs are still hot and sizzling.

classic basil pesto

2 cups loosely packed basil leaves

2 tablespoons pine nuts

2 garlic cloves

2 tablespoons olive oil

4 tablespoons unsalted butter, softened

10 oz. freshly grated Parmesan cheese, ⅔ cup

freshly ground black pepper

SERVES 4

Melt over hot pasta or rice dishes, or serve as an accompaniment to grilled vegetables. Toast the pine nuts in a dry skillet until golden for a variation of this vibrant basil sauce.

Put the basil, pine nuts, and garlic in a food processor and process until finely chopped. Add the oil, butter, Parmesan, and freshly ground black pepper to taste. Process briefly until blended.

Home-made broth is better for making risotto or soup because it gives the best flavor. Make a broth with whatever fresh vegetables are available, then refrigerate or freeze until needed.

vegetable broth

3 tablespoons unsalted butter

1 tablespoon olive oil

3 garlic cloves, crushed

1 large onion, chopped

4 leeks, chopped

2 carrots, chopped

2 celery stalks, chopped

1 fennel bulb, chopped

a handful of fresh flat-leaf parsley, chopped

2 dried bay leaves

2 sprigs of thyme

MAKES ABOUT 4 CUPS

Melt the butter and oil in a large, heavy saucepan. Add the garlic, sauté for 2 minutes, then add the remaining ingredients. Cook, stirring constantly, until softened but not browned.

Add 2½ quarts of water and bring to a boil. Reduce the heat, cover, and simmer for 1½ hours. Let cool.

Return the pan to the heat and simmer for 15 minutes. Strain the broth and return to the pan. Discard the solids. Boil rapidly until reduced by half, then use as needed or let cool and keep in the refrigerator for up to 3 days.

dijon dressing

A simple, all-purpose dressing for salads. You can play around with this as much as you like. Try whole-grain mustard in place of smooth, and try different vinegars—sherry, cider, red wine, or even Japanese rice vinegar.

1 tablespoon smooth Dijon mustard

1 tablespoon white wine vinegar

¼ cup extra virgin olive oil

1 garlic clove, crushed

sea salt and freshly ground black pepper

SERVES 4

Put the mustard, vinegar, oil, and garlic in a bowl and mix with a fork or small balloon whisk.

Add enough water for the consistency you want—about 1–2 tablespoons—and salt and black pepper to taste.

Any leftover dressing can be stored in a screwtop jar in the refrigerator.

fresh red pepper jam

Superb with pasta or on top of toasted bread with shavings of cheese.

2 tablespoons olive oil

2 red bell peppers, halved, seeded, and thinly sliced

2 yellow bell peppers, halved, seeded, and thinly sliced

2 orange bell peppers, halved, seeded, and thinly sliced

1 red chile, halved, seeded, and thinly sliced diagonally

2 garlic cloves, peeled

1 tablespoon sugar

1 lemon, halved

sea salt and freshly ground black pepper

SERVES 4

Heat the oil in a large saucepan. Add the peppers, chile, garlic, and sugar. Squeeze the lemon juice into the pan, then add the squeezed halves. Stir.

Put a piece of wet, crumpled wax paper on top of the mixture in the pan and cover with a lid. Cook gently over low heat for 35–40 minutes until the peppers are meltingly soft. Remove the paper from the pan and increase the heat to reduce the liquid for about 3–4 minutes. Add salt and pepper to taste and remove from the heat. When cool, transfer to sterilized jars. Keep refrigerated and use within 1–2 weeks.

index

conversion charts

Weights and measures have been rounded up
or down slightly to make measuring easier.

Volume equivalents:

American	Metric	Imperial
1 teaspoon	5 ml	
1 tablespoon	15 ml	
¼ cup	60 ml	2 fl.oz.
⅓ cup	75 ml	2½ fl.oz.
½ cup	125 ml	4 fl.oz.
⅔ cup	150 ml	5 fl.oz. (¼ pint)
¾ cup	175 ml	6 fl.oz.
1 cup	250 ml	8 fl.oz.

Weight equivalents:

Imperial	Metric
1 oz.	25 g
2 oz.	50 g
3 oz.	75 g
4 oz.	125 g
5 oz.	150 g
6 oz.	175 g
7 oz.	200 g
8 oz. (½ lb.)	250 g
9 oz.	275 g
10 oz.	300 g
11 oz.	325 g
12 oz.	375 g
13 oz.	400 g
14 oz.	425 g
15 oz.	475 g
16 oz. (1 lb.)	500 g
2 lb.	1 kg

Measurements:

Inches	Cm
¼ inch	5 mm
½ inch	1 cm
¾ inch	1.5 cm
1 inch	2.5 cm
2 inches	5 cm
3 inches	7 cm
4 inches	10 cm
5 inches	12 cm
6 inches	15 cm
7 inches	18 cm
8 inches	20 cm
9 inches	23 cm
10 inches	25 cm
11 inches	28 cm
12 inches	30 cm

Oven temperatures:

110°C	(225°F)	Gas ¼
120°C	(250°F)	Gas ½
140°C	(275°F)	Gas 1
150°C	(300°F)	Gas 2
160°C	(325°F)	Gas 3
180°C	(350°F)	Gas 4
190°C	(375°F)	Gas 5
200°C	(400°F)	Gas 6
220°C	(425°F)	Gas 7
230°C	(450°F)	Gas 8
240°C	(475°F)	Gas 9

credits

Photographs